A Man of his Word

The life of Alastair Hetherington

A Man of his Word

The life of Alastair Hetherington

Edited by Kenneth Roy

Carrick Publishing

First published in 1998 by Carrick Publishing Ltd
2/1 Galt House
31 Bank Street
Irvine KA12 OLL

British Cataloguing-in-Publication Data
A catalogue record for this book is available on request from the British Library.

ISBN 0 946724 40 7

Printed and bound in Great Britain by print in black, Bath

Contents

Milestones

1919	born Llanishen, Glamorganshire, 31 October
1938	becomes student at Corpus Christi College, Oxford
1942	commissioned Royal Armoured Corps
1946	joins *Glasgow Herald*
1950	joins *Manchester Guardian* as defence correspondent
1953	appointed assistant editor and foreign editor
1956	appointed editor
1957	marries Miranda (marriage dissolved, 1978)
1960	appointed member, Royal Commission on the Police
1966	saves *Guardian* from merger with *Times*
1970	Journalist of the Year, National Press Awards
1973	appointed visiting fellow, Nuffield College, Oxford
1975	appointed controller, BBC Scotland (resigns, 1978)
1979	appointed manager, BBC Highland (retires, 1980) marries Sheila
1981	publishes *Guardian Years*
1982	appointed research professor in media studies, Stirling University (retires, 1989) begins producing documentaries for Channel 4 (until 1989)
1984	appointed chairman, Scott Trust (retires, 1989)
1985	publishes *News, Newspapers and Television*
1989	publishes *News in the Regions* edits *Highlands and Islands: a generation of progress*
1990	publishes *Cameras in the Commons* (co-author)
1992	publishes *Inside BBC Scotland 1975-80*
1995	publishes *A Walker's Guide to Arran*

Alastair has known Kenneth Roy for many years as a colleague in BBC Scotland. More recently we have both known him well as a friend: enjoyed his company, admired his writing, been constantly entertained by his dry, sometimes devastating, sense of humour. When he telephoned to ask me if I thought it would be a good idea to produce a book in honour of Alastair, I was delighted, both by the idea and by the generosity of spirit that prompted it. I thank him most warmly, as I do each one of our distinguished contributors: all cherished friends and members of the family, who have taken time and trouble to write about Alastair as they knew him. I have not read these pieces yet, nor shall I until they are published, but I look forward to holding the book in my hands and to sharing it with Alastair. – Sheila Hetherington

I welcome the idea of a book recording Alastair's professional life and achievements and including some childhood memories from the family.

We met in the summer of 1956 when the Suez crisis was unfolding, and when the clarity of thought and the courage which made him an outstanding journalist were dramatically in evidence. One vivid memory is the night in August when Eden addressed the nation, watched in the one small T.V. room on the Manchester Guardian's famous corridor by what seemed like the entire staff. As the Prime Minister stopped speaking, Alastair was vaulting over a desk and seconds later his typewriter keys were clattering, making mincemeat of the Government's position.

The same qualities of clarity and decisiveness again proved critical at a turning point in the Guardian's history in 1966, which was known to few at the time and is perhaps not yet widely understood. On returning from a brief foreign visit he learned that in his absence the Scott Trust had been convened and had, however reluctantly, been persuaded that the Guardian had no independent future because of its financial situation and should merge with the Times. He immediately went into overdrive, throwing the full force of his energy and intellect into marshalling the facts and arguments. Trustees came to the house in Blackheath for briefing and discussion and left with lighter steps, their sinews stiffened for the fight. A few days later the Trust reconvened and reversed its decision. At all costs the paper should be retained in its integrity. I have no doubt that in those few days in November, 1966, during which I lost four pounds, Alastair was personally responsible for the Guardian's survival. – Miranda Beavis

Notes on Contributors

Angus Mitchell, CB, CVO, MC, was born in 1924 and educated at Brasenose College, Oxford. In 1949 he joined the Scottish Office and was latterly Secretary, Scottish Education Department.

Sheila Hetherington has been married to Alastair for almost twenty years and has helped him with research for books and films. She is the author of a biography of the Duchess of Atholl, Scotland's first woman MP (*Katharine Atholl: Against the Tide*).

John Grigg, FRSL, was born in 1924 and educated at Eton and New College, Oxford. He was a columnist with the *Guardian*, 1960-70. He won the Whitbread Award in 1978 for his biography of Lloyd George and wrote Volume VI of the history of the *Times*.

Anthony Howard, CBE, has been obituaries editor of the *Times* since 1993. Born in 1934, he was educated at Christ Church, Oxford, and was president of the Oxford Union, 1955, before being called to the Bar. He was editor of the *New Statesman*, 1972-78, and of the *Listener*, 1979-81, and deputy editor of the *Observer*, 1981-88. He edited the diaries of Richard Crossman.

Jean Stead was a *Guardian* reporter, 1962-67, deputy news editor to John Cole, 1967-70, news editor and assistant editor, 1970-78, assistant editor, special features, 1979-83, and Scottish correspondent, 1983-88. She is now retired.

Sir Peter Gibbings has been chairman of the Radio Authority since 1995. He was born in 1929 and educated at Rugby and Wadham College, Oxford. He was called to the Bar, 1953, and joined the *Observer*, 1960. In 1967 he became managing director of Guardian Newspapers Ltd., and was chairman of Guardian and Manchester Evening News plc, 1973-88.

Peter Preston was born in 1938 and educated at St John's College, Oxford. He entered journalism on the *Liverpool Daily Post*, 1960, and joined the *Guardian*, 1963. He was editor of the *Guardian*, 1975-95.

Adam Raphael is a writer with the *Economist*. He was born in 1938 and educated at Oriel College, Oxford. In 1965 he joined the *Guardian* as a reporter. He was political editor of the *Observer*, 1981-86, and executive editor, 1988-93, presenting *Newsnight* on BBC Television, 1987-88.

Linda Christmas runs the post-graduate newspaper course at City University, London. She joined the *Guardian*, 1971, from the *Times Educational Supplement* and edited Guardian Miscellany, 1973-75.

Ian Mackenzie is a Church of Scotland minister. Born in 1931, he was educated at Fettes and Edinburgh University. He was head of religious programmes, BBC Scotland, 1973-89.

Thomas Prag is managing director of Moray Firth Radio in Inverness. Born in 1947, he was educated at Brasenose College, Oxford. He joined the BBC as a studio manager, 1968.

Tom Nossiter is emeritus professor of government at the LSE and visiting professor of politics at Leeds University. He is a former dean of the graduate school at the LSE. His work includes studies of Indian Communism and nineteenth-century British history.

Philip Schlesinger has been professor of film and media studies at Stirling University since 1989. He was born in 1948 and educated at Queen's College, Oxford, and the LSE. He was professor of sociology, University of Greenwich, 1987-89.

C. Kay Weaver is a lecturer in film and television studies at the University of Waikato, New Zealand. She was educated at Stirling University, where she later worked as a research assistant.

Sir Kenneth Alexander was born in 1922 and educated at Dundee School of Economics. He was principal of Stirling University, 1981-86, chairman of Govan Shipbuilders, 1974-76, chairman of the Highlands and Islands Development Board, 1976-80, and chairman of the Edinburgh Book Festival, 1987-91.

Lucy Hetherington, third of Alastair and Miranda Hetherington's four children, lives in London and produces current affairs programmes for BBC TV.

Tom Hetherington, oldest of the children, recently moved to London as finance manager, London Studios, LWT, after eight years at Yorkshire Television in Leeds.

Mary Hetherington, youngest of the children, has taught languages in Spain, England, and (most recently) Brazil.

Alex Hetherington, second of the children, is a secondary school teacher, living in Hertfordshire.

Foreword

Angus Mitchell

It has been my good fortune to know Alastair for over fifty years in a wide variety of settings – army, journalism, broadcasting, university, hill-walking and family. Others will write with deeper knowledge of Alastair's notable achievements in each of these fields, whereas I can testify to his remarkable adaptability to meet the challenges of diverse occupations.

I first met him in 1943, when he was a lieutenant in the 2nd Northamptonshire Yeomanry commanding a troop of Cromwell tanks. His father (Sir Hector Hetherington, principal of Glasgow University) and mother had been students in Glasgow with my father, so Sir Hector came to visit my parents in Hampshire while Alastair's regiment was stationed nearby.

Alastair appreciated my mother's good cooking (army diet was then less creative than now), and managed to steer his tanks in her direction in several training exercises, one of which coincided with my own leave from the army. As a mere trooper in a training regiment, newly out of school, I was naturally inspired by Alastair (no doubt unconsciously on his part) to follow his footsteps in the Royal Armoured Corps. The Second Front was imminent – an exciting time for young soldiers, but an anxious time for their families.

Alastair's regiment was part of the 11th Armoured Division, which landed in Normandy about two weeks after D-Day and fought bravely for the capture of Caen. In July 1944 his regiment suffered such heavy losses in "Operation Goodwood" south of the city that it had to be disbanded. Alastair was not the only one who thought that this operation had been badly planned, but for him at least there was a happy outcome: he was quickly picked out to serve as intelligence officer in the headquarters of 11th Armoured Division, where he continued until the end of the war. (Staff jobs of this kind were greatly envied by soldiers at the front, but were not quite as safe as many supposed; one of his more exciting exploits is described elsewhere in this volume, in his own words.)

By this time I was serving in another regiment in the same armoured division, and was thus able to meet him occasionally in Belgium, Holland and Germany as we advanced to the Danish frontier. I well remember having lunch with him in a beautiful castle at Plon in Schleswig, when we were disarming the defeated Wehrmacht in the summer of 1945. Shortly after that he was transferred to Hamburg to start a German newspaper, a fitting beginning for his distinguished career in journalism.

Our paths did not cross again for nearly thirty years, although I heard good reports of Alastair's progress from his brother Scott, one of my colleagues in the Scottish Office. In 1975 I was agreeably surprised to hear from Alastair that he was leaving the *Guardian* to become controller of BBC Scotland, and would like to stay with us in Edinburgh before taking up his new post. It was good to meet Miranda and their children for the first time, to hear more about his work on the *Guardian*, and to learn of his ideas on the future of broadcasting. Apart from our personal and social network, we also had some official contacts because of my department's interest in school broadcasting.

Not many Scots would share the opinion of the late Sir David English that Alastair was "mad" to leave the *Guardian* and go to BBC Scotland. It soon became clear, however, that some of Alastair's proposals for Scotland did not find favour with BBC headquarters in London, and that the level of autonomy he had been expecting would not in practice be forthcoming. One cannot help wondering whether things might have turned out differently if a Scottish Assembly had been set up as expected in 1979. Some people were surprised by Alastair's decision to "step down" to the post of manager of BBC Highland, but he obviously enjoyed this chance to foster local initiatives, especially in the Northern and Western Isles. He gave us a racy account of this period in *Inside BBC Scotland 1975-80.*

Our careers intermeshed once again in 1984, when I was appointed to the Court of Stirling University; Alastair was already serving there as research professor in media studies, and as one of his "employers" I heard nothing but praise for his work in this new field of academic development. It is good to know that the work of this department of the university has continued to prosper since Alastair retired.

After all these happy contacts over the years, our relationship has now started a new chapter. In the last year or two it has been sad to see the progressive deterioration in Alastair's memory, his inability to recognise old friends and the clouding of his sharp intellect. It is reassuring, however, to find him as warm-hearted and courteous as ever, and to know that he is receiving devoted support from Sheila, his family and the services available.

As a trustee of the dementia centre at Stirling University, I am painfully aware not only of the serious gaps in services for people with dementia, but of the stigma still attached to this disease by many members of the public. Ronald Reagan's brave statement about his own dementia has done much to reduce this stigma, which has often made the families concerned reluctant to seek the help they need. Let us likewise pay tribute to Alastair's family for their readiness to follow that good example, by sharing their knowledge of his disability with all his friends and colleagues. The contributions which follow betoken the gratitude and affection which have been earned by this remarkable Scotsman.

Part I

About Alastair

Beginnings

Sheila Hetherington

The Reids

Alastair's parents both lived in the Hillfoots, the string of small towns lying at the foot of the Ochil Hills in central Scotland: Menstrie, Alva, Tillicoultry and Dollar. The Ochils, beautiful, treeless and desolate, almost uninhabited but for flocks of black-faced sheep, spread northwards for twenty miles or so into Perthshire, and come to an abrupt end above the Hillfoots, providing each little town with a glen of great beauty leading through a steep escarpment, with swift, abundant falls of soft water that made them ideal for large turn-of-the-century woollen mills. Those mills, together with farming and coal-mining on the flat plain below, supported a fairly prosperous population.

The coal mines fell out of use many years ago, their old bings removed long since. Most of the mills have been converted into flats and there is a museum. New housing has eaten into the fertile farmlands. Yet the long, straight, grey-stone main streets passing through the four little towns remain much the same as they were in 1900, when the Hetherington family lived in Tillicoultry and (unknown to each other) the Reids three miles to the west, in Alva.

Neither the Hetheringtons nor the Reids had their beginnings in those Hillfoots villages, however. Both were Border families. Alastair's grandfather, William Reid, was born at Troqueer, near Dumfries, in 1861. William's mother, Marion Dickson, was a cousin of the writer Samuel Crockett, whose novels are little remembered and probably seldom read today, though in his time he was almost as popular and as much enjoyed as his friend J.M. Barrie. William's father Samuel was an ornamental stonemason in Maxwelltown, his grandfather William a surgeon in Moniaive, Dumfriesshire; surgeon William's father (who would have been Alastair's great-great-great grandfather), born about 1747, lived in Dumfries and was said to have been a friend of Robert Burns during the last five years of the poet's life.

Grandfather Reid went to Glasgow University and on to Dundas Vale teacher training college. In his graduation photograph he gazes at the photographer quizzically: a pleasant-looking young man, clean-shaven but for a short dark beard that began and ended underneath his chin. At Dundas William fell in love with a fellow student: a pretty, intelligent and humorous girl called Jessie Hunter. Jessie's forebears had been farmers on the island of Cumbrae, a mile or so off the Ayrshire mainland at Largs. Every day of their lives, the Hunters must have looked westwards from their fields at Craigenower Farm across the water to the jagged hills of the island of Arran that dominates the Clyde estuary, where generations later Alastair made his home.

Andrew Hunter, the farmer's son, went to sea, became skipper of a sloop, and was drowned in Dunure harbour. His wife Margaret died three months later, leaving seven orphaned children to be separated and shared out amongst friends and relations. One of the sons, Robert, was already of an age to begin work of some kind, but farming and the sea were impossible as he had been lame from birth, so he was apprenticed to a shoe manufacturer in Dalry, Ayrshire. Years later, when the owner retired, Robert took over his business, prospered, and married Mary Whiteford from the Garnock valley, daughter of a "pioneer" of Ayrshire silk embroidery.

William went on to teach in Falkirk (testimonials refer to him as "an excellent teacher, a good disciplinarian, and a thorough gentleman") while Jessie was appointed head teacher at Kippen, twenty five miles away; but they possessed bicycles, and the romance prospered. They were married in 1886 and Alastair's mother Alison was born in the schoolhouse at Airth, where William was now headmaster, the following year. In 1888, William – still only twenty-seven – became rector of Alva Academy. Two boys and three more girls were born. A last son, Alan, was born after the family had moved to Shettleston, William now being rector of Eastwood Academy. Alison was already twenty and studying in France.

William's departure from Alva occasioned a large presentation party, during which many eloquent speeches of farewell were made. According to the *Hillfoots Record*, Miss Drummond was called upon to sing "The Flight of Ages", which she did with marked expression and feeling. Miss Couper of Menstrie – also with marked expression – sang "When the Heart is Young".

The new home at Shettleston was called Bertrohill: a square stone house overlooking peaceful farmland. Both house and farmland have been swallowed up by a voracious Glasgow, but Alastair (aged I suppose about four or five) had a vivid childhood recollection of it. To his huge enjoyment Bertrohill suffered a devastating flood – the cause of which he did not know – while he was there. A great tidal wave rushed in through the back door and out through the front, carrying all before it.

The Reid family went to Glasgow's High Schools. They would all run for the train each morning and occupy an entire compartment; occasionally the train would wait for a family straggler. Six of the seven went on to Glasgow University: the girls (Alison, Jessie, Winnie) to become teachers, Howard an engineer, Arnold a minister, Alan a doctor. Alison and Winnie both graduated with first-class honours. Adina (Dine) also qualified as a teacher.

A family photograph exists of Jessie and William, surrounded by their family, taken in 1919 in front of Bertrohill. Alastair had not yet been born, but his parents, Hector and Alison, are there. Arnold, handsome and upright in army uniform. His wife May, with their first child, Margot, on her knee. Howard is in army uniform too. Jessie, Winnie and Dine, prim and pretty in the calf-length dresses of the day. Alan, eleven, stands in front. Alastair's brother Scott and cousin Micky stand, solemn, small and sturdy in smocked sailor suits.

Howard joined the Glasgow steel firm of Stewarts and Lloyds and moved to South Africa. Arnold became a minister, first in Whithorn and later in Selkirk. His children were of a similar age or younger than Scott and Alastair. Arnold's second daughter, Kathleen, married the Scottish rugby hero and sometime president of the SRU, Charlie Drummond. Her brother Alastair is the writer, translator and poet Alastair Reid, who divides his time between New York and the Dominican Republic. Jessie was widowed during the war; her son Micky died of meningitis. Winnie became a teacher at Glasgow Academy, Dine at Park School.

Like so many women of her generation, Winnie had lost someone she loved in the war, and put thoughts of marriage out of her mind. To her own surprise, in early middle age she met and married Dr Archie Hyslop, an Aberdonian classics scholar and director of education for the Borders. (Archie, a shy bachelor of forty-nine, first encountered her in her classroom at Glasgow Academy. At that moment it crossed his mind to ask her to marry him, but he decided against doing so in the presence of twenty five nine-year-old boys. In any case he was to receive several gentle rebuffs before Winnie succumbed.) Archie had several other hats – he was an accomplished musician; author of most of the songs in the repertoire of the famous Scottish comedian Harry Gordon; and a connoisseur and lover of art. Many of the great Scottish artists of the day were Archie's friends and companions, and over the years of his bachelorhood he amassed a wonderful collection of the work of the Colourists – mainly Peploes, but Hunter, Gillies and others were included.

The marriage took place in July 1942, and Winnie joined Archie in his lovely home overlooking the River Tweed in Melrose. It was a love-match. For a few months they were tenderly happy; but that Christmas Archie became ill. A brain tumour was diagnosed and he died in February 1943. Winnie, devastated, survived him by fifty years, living on in the old home, with Archie's housekeeper as companion. To visit Tweed House was always a joy: for the delight of Winnie herself, and for the viewing of the paintings; we were always conscious of the privilege of visiting a private, secret gallery. Each summer in later years, when her housekeeper had her annual holiday, Alastair would go down to Melrose to be with Winnie, to make their meals, and to spend days walking in the Eildon hills. In 1989 Winnie asked for Alastair's help in finding the most suitable place to leave the paintings, in her husband's name. Because of Archie's Aberdeen connection, Alastair approached the director of the city art gallery, who gladly accepted the promise of the glory to come, and on Winnie's death in June 1993, some thirty six paintings were received by the gallery: the Hyslop Collection.

It was the Reid grandparents who began the family love affair with Arran which has lasted now for five generations. Sometime in the 1890s the Reid family began to spend a month each summer on Arran, always renting a roomy stone farmhouse in the clachan of Thundergay, which looks across the Kilbrannon Sound to the low hills of Kintyre. The children loved the freedom and strangeness of that month spent amongst the Gaelic-speaking inhabitants of the clachan; ran wild; were greatly in awe of old Mr Currie, the Clachar (head of the community); and gave an annual concert in the barn before they left.

No one speaks the Arran form of Gaelic any longer, but Thundergay today is much as it was then, the farmhouse and half-dozen or so whitewashed cottages sitting undisturbed along the hillside, hens, dogs, cats and children running freely through unenclosed gardens, the sea below merging almost imperceptibly with the grey-blue sky. Recollections of those holidays on Arran drew Alison and her brother Arnold to return to the island again and again, bringing their own families back to it every year. Alastair was nine months old when he was first brought to a cottage on the Newton shore in Lochranza, and the island cast its spell on him. Now it draws his children, and their children in turn.

The Hetheringtons

Hetheringtons are probably of Norse-Viking stock. Hoderings – Hoder's people – may have sailed their longship up the Solway Firth about a thousand years ago and made their way a few miles beyond the bog and marshland that surrounded its shores, settling on land near what is now Brampton. The historian George MacDonald Fraser (author of *The Steel Bonnets*) has found that in the sixteenth century Hetheringtons were concentrated between Hethersgill and Triermain, close to Hadrian's Wall. What seems certain is that they were part of the wild reiving fraternity that in mediaeval and English Tudor times fought and pillaged across the disputed lands that were neither part of England nor of Scotland. These included the powerful Elliots, Armstrongs, Maxwells and Jardines, who lived and acted as they wished, regarding themselves as subservient to no king, no law, no authority.

The Hetheringtons seem to have maintained a safely low profile, acting as agents and gatherers of rents (sometimes of blackmail) on behalf of those senior Border families. George has said that unlike the more thrusting families, who swelled their ranks and strength by absorbing others under their family name, the Hetheringtons remained a close family group, so that probably all present-day Hetheringtons share a common ancestry.

Their instinct for self-preservation in those early days may have had the unexpected effect of preserving their distinctive genes. According to George, they are often tall and rangy, fair-haired, with hazel or blue eyes, a prominent nose, and a great deal of personal charm. In 1995, we arranged to hold a Hetherington Gathering at Lanercost Priory. About a hundred people came – from America, Australia, Ireland, England, Wales and Scotland – and George's description of their physique was uncannily accurate. The last recorded account of a Hetherington family gathering took place in 1569, when they apparently came together to plan the murder of the bishop of Carlisle.

For six generations at least, Alastair's direct forebears lived only fifteen miles to the west of Brampton, on the Scottish side of the present border, on the Solway Firth. Here Hector Hetherington, blacksmith of Clarencefield, begat Joseph Hetherington. Joseph Hetherington begat Hector Hetherington, who begat Thomas Hetherington. Thomas Hetherington begat Hector Hetherington, Alastair's father.

The first-mentioned Hector was an elder of the lovely church of Ruthwell, and was present, with his son Joseph, on that melancholy occasion when Robert Burns came to the manse to take tea with the minister and his wife. Burns was dying, and had been misguidedly advised to come from Dumfries to the Solway for some days, to bathe in the sea water at a tidal well near Clarencefield. The shock of the sudden surge of extremely cold water on his frail, fevered body had accelerated his end, as he was sadly aware. That afternoon, sitting in the sunny parlour at Ruthwell manse, the minister's wife made to close the blinds to shade her guest, but Burns begged her to leave them, declaring that he had but a short time left to enjoy the light.

Joseph Hetherington joined his father as blacksmith on the main street at Clarencefield, and in time the business passed on to his son, Hector. Smithing seems to have been the family tradition, for Hetherington blacksmiths were to be found all round Dumfriesshire as the family grew and spread. Perhaps it is not too fanciful to speculate that Hetherington ancestors had been forgers of the reivers' steel bonnets and swords. These village smiddies were thriving and important businesses, for the livelihood of a community depended heavily on the work of the blacksmith. The forge was a convivial meeting place in every town or village and the smith was a prosperous man. According to his obituary in the local paper, Joseph was also a well-educated man with a gift for story-telling.

Further north, at Lockerbie, Joseph's brother and sons were also in the trade. But nearby, up among the rolling hills at Moffat, another brother, Thomas, had become the local pharmacist. The Clarencefield smiddy being already spoken for by the eldest of Joseph's grandsons, the second grandson – also Thomas – was apprenticed to his uncle, about 1882. Uncle Thomas's shop remains in Moffat today, under the same name, but different ownership. Thomas senior devised a recipe for lavender water; here, and only here in all the world, Thomas

Hetherington's lavender water may still be purchased.

His training with his uncle complete, Thomas the younger married Helen Mundell of Tundergarth, and found a post as chemist's assistant in Cowdenbeath. Here their first son, Hector, Alastair's father, was born in 1888. Two years later Thomas bought the chemist's shop in Tillicoultry in the Hillfoots, and here a second son, George, and a daughter, Marie, were born. Unusually, the chemist's business was combined with the post office, within a substantial, well-proportioned stone building. The family home was above the shop, its wide windows looking up towards Tillicoultry Glen and the hills beyond. Thomas, chemist, postmaster and Justice of the Peace, who also became something of an authority on the subject of education, was a much-respected man o' pairts.

Young Hector, Alastair's father, attended Tillicoultry School until he was thirteen. Of his schooling there, he wrote later that in some ways he was not well educated for his age. Some might disagree with him, for he comments that by the age of thirteen he had read no imaginative literature of any consequence, knew little of Britain's history, or of music or science. But he knew "quite thoroughly" the accidence and syntax of the English language and "so far as I had then gone, of Latin and French as well...I was good in Arithmetic and in the elements of Geometry and Algebra, and knew my Catechism by heart, as certainly as had all my ancestors for a hundred years or more. It had the same status as the multiplication table and we entertained no doubts whatever about the equal validity of both."

If Hector had thought himself under-educated at Tillicoultry School, Dollar Academy, in its elegant Palladian building three miles east of Tillicoultry, repaired any omissions and opened up intellectual horizons and challenges for him during the next five years. He left Dollar as dux in 1905, winning a bursary to Glasgow University with the intention (encouraged by his parents) of becoming a minister of the United Free Church. There he gained a double first in economic science and philosophy, followed by a second in classics, winning an additional fellowship and scholarship.

None of this academic brilliance turned Hector into a "stuffy" young man. He was certainly of a serious turn of mind, but

Alastair has commented that his father had an endearing, boyish sense of fun and was a marvellous man and a splendid father. Throughout his life he remained modest, wise, cheerful, ever-approachable to sons, colleagues and students alike: a man of great warmth and immense personal charm.

As a student, Hector lived at the university settlement for Possil. The Edwardian years were times of terrible hardship for some of Glasgow's population, which included some of the poorest and most deprived people in Britain, many living in appalling conditions. The aim of the settlement was social rehabilitation – providing food, shelter and basic clothing for the down-and-outs, visiting the local sick, and generally helping those in need: they did not have far to look for clients.

Hector's closest friends were fellow students Walter Elliot, a medical student who became a Scottish Conservative MP and pre-war minister, and another medical student, Osborne Mavor, who would also become famous as the playwright James Bridie. These three rented a spartan, remote cottage between Fintry and Lennoxtown in the Campsie Hills, and went out there at weekends to tramp through the long glens during the days and hammer out their philosophies in discussion by the fire in the evenings. (It was said of Elliot, though the story is probably apocryphal, that as a young doctor just after the first world war, he received a telegram from his home town of Lanark, asking him to stand for parliament, to which he replied, "Yes. Which party?")

After graduating, Hector became warden of Possil settlement and joined the university staff as a junior lecturer in philosophy. Meantime Alison Reid was studying for her first-class honours degree in modern languages, which included a year in Osnabruck and Saumur. She and Hector had once met casually as fellow students, and by some stroke of fate they met again a year or two later. They fell in love, though Hector later said, with a cheerful grin, that with so many beautiful sisters to choose from, it had been a remarkably difficult decision to make. They were well matched, with similar backgrounds, keen minds and a dry sense of humour.

Both Hector and Alison believed – it had been instilled into them by their own parents, and they in turn instilled it into their sons – that a sound education laid the foundation for life; and that it was essential to have a personal goal. Achievement of that goal depended on dedication and hard work. These attitudes, of course, reflected both their times and backgrounds. The Hetherington and Reid families were steeped in a staunch, unquestioning Presbyterian faith combined with a politically Liberal outlook.

Alison and Hector were married in 1914. It was to be a long and happy marriage. Their lives revolved round each other, and many people have said that without Lady Hetherington's support and presence, Sir Hector could not have achieved all that he did.

Hector volunteered for the army in 1914, but was rejected because of short-sightedness and instead became a lecturer at Sheffield University. A year later, at the age of twenty-seven, he was appointed to the chair of logic and philosophy at University College, Cardiff: which is where, at Llanishen, on All Hallow's Eve 1919, (Hector) Alastair was born.

Childhood

In spite of his Welsh birth, Alastair has always believed himself to be a Scotsman – or, as he wrote firmly in his diary at the age of six: "We are Scotch". He could hardly count himself a Welshman, for he was only three months old when the family moved from Cardiff (Hector having accepted an appointment as principal and professor of philosophy at University College, Exeter), nor an Englishman, as he was only four when the family returned to Scotland – or, in Alastair's case, went there for the first time. Hector had inherited the chair of moral philosophy first occupied in 1728 by the illustrious scholar Francis Hutcheson.

The Hetheringtons lived in one of the professors' houses – number one on the quad; and in the autumn of 1924 Alastair began his education as a pupil at Park School. This was a private girls' school, but there was a sprinkling of small boys in the infant department. He was delivered there each morning by a maid, but was allowed to return home across Kelvin Park in the afternoon by himself – or more often in the company of his first girlfriend, Ruth. Together they wandered happily along the complex of paths that criss-cross the park, pausing to play by the fountain or on the swings.

Alastair loved his parents equally, though differently. His mother was, to him, beautiful and fun, and she in her turn indulged him a little. His father was kind, wise, totally dependable, and careful to avoid spoiling either of his sons. Alastair could never remember his father losing his temper, but social injustice in all its forms aroused Hector's fiery indignation.

The pathetic, sometimes ghastly, sights that he – a well-fed, well-bred young man from a fairly prosperous rural background – had seen at the settlement influenced his outlook for ever more; and that, in turn, Alastair's own. But Hector never forgot his rural roots in the Scottish border country – an awareness that Scott and Alastair also inherited.

Alison was perhaps more perjink, more conscious of her position at the heart of Glasgow society, but Alastair, like his father, would rejoice cheerfully: "I'm a pleb!" Hector taught his sons to believe in the fundamental right of all people to live in dignity, however simply. At the same time he emphasised that individual rights could not, and should not, be unconditional: "Society owes no rights, no duty, to any man, save that he has the chance to be a man and play his part. No one may cast his burden on others unless he is ready to take his share in the common load. He has no title to benefits unless, according to his power, he pays the cost."

Years later, when Alastair was perhaps eleven or twelve, his father would take him with him on his missions to deprived areas of the city. The sight of disconsolate groups of unemployed men during the depression of the early '30s left a deep and lasting impression on him. He remembered being taken to Clydebank, to see a great Cunarder. "It was under construction, but all work on it had stopped. The grey hull towered above the shipyard, silent and desolate. But what struck me most were the drab groups of men gathered together in the streets outside, unemployed and dispirited, with nothing to do and nowhere to go. It was a profoundly sad, disturbing sight."

He could also remember the general strike quite vividly. He was only six, and of course he did not understand the issues. It seemed to him to be a time of high excitement, and he was impressed to find that his father began to take him to and from school himself: concerned, no doubt, that he might be caught up in one of the demonstrations that seemed to take place near the tramway terminus outside the university.

Head-hunting was not an expression then used, but whatever it might be called, it kept happening to Hector. In 1927 he was invited to become vice-chancellor of Liverpool University: an offer not to be refused lightly, but it must have been hard for Alastair's parents to decide to uproot the family yet again and leave Glasgow. After long consideration, Hector accepted the summons from Liverpool, painfully aware that this move would now mean abandoning philosophy for ever. This decision may have been because he believed that he was better at administration than philosophy – though this was not true. He was a first-class administrator, but in making his choice, philosophy lost a very gifted mind. He was a superb writer, and now the great philosophical treatise he had planned as the culmination of his academic work would remain unwritten.

Off they went again – another upheaval. They went to live in Croxteth, where Alastair went to a new school and made new friends, and though he missed Glasgow, Liverpool had its own fascination for an eight-year-old. There were many similarities between the two cities. There was the wide river, the sea not far off, docks and great liners. A friend of Hector's arranged permission for Alastair to visit the docks whenever he wanted to go. His parents were not worried for his safety, and to his satisfaction he was allowed to wander there by himself.

Alastair did not stay long at the school in Croxteth. When he was ten he was sent to the Dragon School in Oxford. This was a school to which Oxford academics sent their sons and daughters, so the standard of teaching was high, as were the results expected. He was not at all unhappy there. Once again there were new friends, new subjects, new occupations. For the the first year or two he enjoyed the academic work, but gradually, and certainly towards the end of his final year, his father began to find his school reports disappointing. He was slipping behind and he couldn't explain the reason.

It took his father's driver to spot the problem. He collected Alastair from the station for the summer vacation, and as usual Alastair sat beside him, chatting amicably and enjoyably. They shared an interest in car numbers and it did not take the driver long to discover that this year he was unable to read the numbers of the cars immediately ahead of them. Delivering him to his father, he told him gruffly: "There's something wrong with the lad's eyes. He can't read." He was right. In those years at the Dragon, Alastair had become short-sighted and needed glasses. As soon as he had them his life changed completely. At the simplest level he had been quite unable to read the school blackboard. Now it was as though a troublesome curtain had been raised, to reveal things that he had not been aware of.

He enjoyed Sundays at the Dragon. They might not have been every small boy's idea of fun – but it meant freedom. After school service he was allowed to take the fifteen-minute walk to the home of an old friend of his parents, Mrs Gerrans. Alastair thinks she was the wife of a don: German, with wispy, wavy, white hair, usually clad in long, dark, silky garments. She was most kind. He was given a large lunch and tea, and allowed to join in conversation with the adult guests. Occasionally she took him out to lunch with some of her friends. Alastair remembered displeasing her only once. It must have been in 1932-33, for he spoke of Hitler's coming to power in Germany. Surely, he said, in his innocence or ignorance, Hitler could not be as bad as the pre-war regime had been? Mrs Gerrans turned on him at once and delivered a lengthy and unforgettable lecture which left him in no doubt as to the loathsome nature of Nazism.

The Dragon encouraged pupils to keep detailed diaries of their summer holidays. From that early Dragon training, keeping an anecdotal house diary has developed into a habit, and there is a collection of diaries compiled by everyone – family and guests – staying at Alastair and Miranda's Lake District farmhouse at Borwick Fold in the 1960s and '70s, and throughout our '80s and '90s years at the cottage in Arran.

The first entry of the first diary begins on the last day of term, July 25, 1930:

> After breakfast I went over to School House with Mr Vassall and Tony Rogers. Tony was going to the station in the school brake. I saw him off, and walked back to Mr Vassall's house. I got my prize, which was a book called "Poems of Goldsmith". I was walking down Charlbury Road when I saw Skipper, so I went in and asked him to put his name in it. A little later Mrs Vassall asked me and J Searle to go and cut some lavender for her. We had just finished cutting the lavender when my Mother and Father arrived to take me home.

Skipper was the headmaster's father. He lived at the school and was a great favourite with the boys. As his name implies, he was a keen sailor and used to take a few of the senior boys sailing to the west coast of Scotland each summer.

A visit to Edinburgh in 1932 with his parents and their friend Richard Armstrong (a lawyer, and treasurer of Liverpool University) shows Alastair to be a child of definite opinions:

> We took a tram back to the art galleries. The Royal Scottish Gallery had a scratch collection of modern pictures and sculptures in it. I thought it was a very good exhibition, and would have liked to study it carefully, but Mr Armstrong was not really interested in it. We then went on to the National Gallery of Scotland, which was full of old pictures. I did not like many of them, except one, which Mr Armstrong thought to be very bad. I thought Gainsborough's pictures rotten, and Mr Armstrong agreed. Raeburn's were not as bad, though not much good. Mr Armstrong liked these, however. He looked at nearly every picture fairly carefully. Luckily there were not a great number.

A picture begins to emerge of a quiet, studious boy, eager to be friendly with his peers, yet also self-sufficient, content to be alone, and perfectly at ease in the company of adults. Although he still saw some of his Croxteth schoolfriends during the holidays, it must have been difficult to maintain friendships. In his short lifetime he had already moved from Exeter to Glasgow to Liverpool to Oxford: and was about to move to Norfolk.

At thirteen, Alastair went to Gresham's School, at Holt, in north Norfolk. His father had chosen it after careful research. Scott, Alastair's brother, had been unhappy at Stowe, and Hector did not intend to repeat that mistake. Gresham's was a school with an excellent, liberal outlook and the teaching was first class.

Alastair enjoyed travelling there, using the cross-country railway journeys between Liverpool and Holt, which could be accomplished using a variety of routes. He regarded it as a personal challenge to discover a new route each time.

Gresham's was, on the whole, a kindly environment. One of the senior prefects at the time was Charles Scott, grandson of the great "CP" of the *Manchester Guardian.* Charles's cousin Richard Scott, who would be chairman of the Scott Trust and a staunch ally throughout Alastair's editorship, had recently left the school.

Years later, as a young journalist on the *Glasgow Herald*, Alastair observed Richard, already an ace correspondent on the *Manchester Guardian*, at a function in London (it was probably the foreign ministers' conference in December, 1947). Richard, handsome, dark and elegant, was seated at a bar stool with a group of fellow top journalists, conversing animatedly, laughing, casually smoking a cigarette through a long black holder. Alastair reflected that he could never aspire to such sophistication.

He settled down easily at Gresham's. In their free time the boys were able to cycle at will round the countryside. It was perfect cycling country. The roads were flat and quiet, and the Norfolk coast and hinterland are very attractive, providing at times a horizon that stretches without interruption round 360 degrees, so that the arching sky in all its moods is the dominant feature.

Alastair was not one of Gresham's great sportsmen by any means. He played a bit of hockey, but despite the family cricket games on Arran, he did not play cricket for his house, still less for the school. Hector had played cricket for his county – Clackmannanshire – and he and Scott were both addicted to golf, which they played very well and often. Hector felt that two hours on the golf course every few days made him a better principal. He had once or twice attempted to introduce Alastair to the game, on holiday in Edzell, but Alastair wrote in his diary that he thought it "too round-shouldered and narrow" compared to hill-walking – he had a change of heart later in life and came to enjoy golf a great deal, though he said it was as much for the scenery as for the game itself.

During their morning break, the boys were able to read a wide selection of newspapers which were laid out for them on the table in the common room. It was there that Alastair first encountered the *Manchester Guardian*, which he admired more than any other, and from that encounter may possibly have formed some hazy idea of a future in journalism.

Here, at last, Alastair was able to make some long-term friendships. Among these was Nigel (now Sir Nigel) Foulkes, with whom he shared a study during his time at the school. There was an active debating society, and a copy of *The Gresham* reports that in October 1937, Nigel Foulkes moved: "That this house deplores the view that schooldays are the best part of life". H.A. Hetherington, opposing the motion, pointed out that anyone who supported the motion did not realise the advantages of school life. He told the house that he could imagine some honourable members longing for their former schooldays when, "after catching the 8.18 every morning, bowlered and bespatted, they had to spend their half-days watching their wives trying on hats".

Youth

In 1936 Alastair's father returned to Glasgow, to his final and most personally rewarding post, which would last for the next quarter of a century. The principal, the historian Sir Robert Rait, had died unexpectedly. Hector Hetherington was appointed to succeed him, and the appointment proved to be an inspiration. His great contribution to Glasgow (and to many other universities as chairman of the committee of British vice-chancellors) brought him a knighthood in 1936, a KBE in 1948 and a GBE on his retirement in 1962. He is said to have been the last principal to have known the names of all the students, and he instituted the custom of sending an annual letter to all graduates giving them news of their old university. The students were delighted by their new principal. He first addressed them at a meeting in the Bute Hall, in the presence of his wife, telling them that, as fellow students at Glasgow, he and his wife had been competitors for a prize awarded annually by the university. "She came first and I came second, and it has been that way ever since," he said, with a twinkle in his eye.

It was a happy return. The Hetheringtons moved back to the quadrangle beside the university chapel, to what was then termed Principal's Lodgings. Alastair loved that house. It was to be his home until he left for Manchester in 1952 – and beyond, for he returned there as often as possible until Sir Hector retired in 1961. From one of the upstairs windows he could see the high peaks of Arran on a clear day – no longer possible because of modern building. A few years ago we both visited the Lodgings at the invitation of Sir William and Lady Fraser – a visit which gave him great pleasure. The house had been altered in shape – now running lengthwise instead of vertically within the long building. The fine reception rooms, Alastair said, were more beautifully decorated and arranged than in his parents' time, and he was able to re-visit the room that had been his bedroom for so many years.

In late August and early September 1936, Alastair went on a walking tour with Lawrence Arnold, a school friend. Principal's Lodgings were being redecorated, though he noted as he left the house that "the awful red wallpaper is still showing" – this presumably a legacy from the Rait occupation. That morning he called on two of his friends, Sam and Angus, university janitors, for a chat, before going into town to meet Lawrence, whom he took for a meal before going to the cinema. Next day they packed their rucksacks and left by train for the Trossachs. The sun was shining, he bought a felt hat and some toothpaste, and they were off. They were sixteen and their parents were content for them to go on a walking tour with no definite itinerary. They took the train to Callander and during the next few days walked westwards towards Loch Lomond, over several fine mountains, including Cruachan and the Cobbler. The weather was hot and they walked, climbed, bathed in lochs, and stayed in a series of comfortable farmhouses.

Alastair had been climbing regularly since he was about ten – he had first climbed Goat Fell in Arran when he was eight – but that summer of 1936 was the beginning of his real passion for hill-walking. He was never tempted to indulge in "Munro-bagging" for its own sake, but he has climbed most of the high hills in Scotland, some of them many times.

Oxford
as recalled by Alastair himself

Autumn 1938. We arrived at Corpus just as the threat of war seemed to have lifted. Our Prime Minister, Hitler, Daladier and Mussolini had met in Munich. Chamberlain had returned, waving his worthless piece of paper. But for a time the nation was fooled. In the country at large there was a sense of relief. Things were going to be all right. The newspapers of the day enthusiastically endorsed this view. The *Glasgow Herald* and the *Manchester Guardian* were among the few papers delivering a more sobering reaction.

Because of my early years at the Dragon School, the buildings, towers, spires and busy streets of Oxford were already familiar, and I looked forward to returning. Corpus was chosen on my father's advice. He had been delighted by my brother Scott's performance there, and felt that I too would benefit from being in a small college. He gave me £300 a year to live on – a generous allowance for those times – and I managed very well on it.

Corpus was wonderful. New freedom, new friends, theatres, magnificent choral music, hockey, walks by the Cherwell and the Isis, and much else. My rooms that year were not of the best, being above the baths and lavatories, but there was plenty of room – and it was mine! After almost ten years of sharing dormitories with about thirty other boys, I found my quarters at Corpus very comfortable. I had brought with me two paintings of Scottish mountains, not of the finest quality, but good enough. Of my scout I remember little, except that he was friendly and helpful. I was not much trouble to him, I hope, nor he to me.

As to Corpus teaching, for me one name stands out: Denis Brogan, the Corpus politics tutor. I had put myself down to read English as my main subject, but first we had to pass through two other hoops. The one that was to matter most to me, though I did not realise it at first, was politics. It took up most of my first two terms.

Brogan drove me hard. At first he frightened me, but I soon got over that. He asked fast and difficult questions, and he expected a quick response. He was sharper and more critical than any of my Gresham's teachers, good though they were – and they were very good. He, like me, came from a Glasgow background, but Brogan had no intention of allowing that to make life any easier for me.

Scott had been under him for three years. He had won a class 1 on PPE, led by Brogan and others, and then, in one further year, just before I came, he had won another class 1 on modern history. Brogan had similar expectations of me, which I was never likely to achieve. But he did me great good, guiding me towards the political journalism that was to become my life. He egged me on, as my father also did, to work for the *Glasgow Herald* the following summer, and again in the summer of 1940. This led to a staff appointment on that newspaper on my return from the army in 1946.

In spite of my new love of politics, English was far from neglected. Corpus did not provide an English tutor and I was taught by H.E.B. Brett-Smith, then university reader in English. Most of his tutorials took place at his home, sometimes with me alone and occasionally with one or two others. He was an elderly man, approaching retirement, quiet and gentle, rarely critical, and almost always responsive and interested in what we said or wrote. When the war came he reorganised the course, since we might be called to military service at any time. So I mercifully skipped Anglo-Saxon and went straight to Shakespeare, John Donne, John Milton and beyond.

For a year or two I thought seriously of becoming an arts journalist. By the time I left the army in 1946 I knew for certain that political journalism was my goal, but at Oxford my developing interest in what might loosely be termed "the arts" led to my involvement in the setting up, in the winter of 1939-40, of the Oxford University Arts Club, with Iris Murdoch of Somerville as chairman, and myself as secretary. Iris was a great stirrer-upper. She was quite bossy and demanding, but she was great to work with and there was a lot of fun in her. In spite of wartime difficulties and restrictions, we were able to prevail upon some notable people in the arts world to come and talk to audiences of at least fifty or sixty – once over a hundred. Our meetings took place, on average every second week, at the Ashmolean.

The autumn of 1938, together with the winter and spring that followed, brought the threat of war even nearer. Informal discussion in the common room and our occasional debates, both at Corpus and at the Union, were serious and full of foreboding. That, at any rate, is my recollection – others may remember debates of a lighter nature.

During our first weeks in Oxford a parliamentary by-election which would test public opinion on the Munich agreement took place. The master of Balliol, A.D. Lindsay, appalled by the abandonment of Czechoslovakia and the implications of appeasement, stood as an independent against the government candidate, Quintin Hogg – Lord Hailsham – a fellow of All Souls: two Oxford men in conflict. For many of us this was our initiation into politics on the ground, as we cheerfully delivered leaflets on behalf of Lindsay. For us it was new and exciting – but the crucial question was how the citizens of Oxford, including industrial Cowley, would vote. In an outcome that accurately reflected the still-pacifist mood of the nation, Hogg won.

The events in Prague the following March (which tragically proved Lindsay's point) were a watershed. From that moment we knew that we were all likely to be swept into war service before long.

One of my most poignant recollections of those years was of early May 1940. I was joint producer and stage manager of a theatre production given by Christ Church and Corpus. The play was T.S. Eliot's *Murder in the Cathedral* and it was performed in the inner quad of Christ Church. On the final day, before the show, I had to meet someone (from Birmingham, I think) at the railway station. As I waited for the train to come, another came in on the northward platform. It was full of wounded British soldiers – the first time I had seen any. It was a pitiful sight, and a dreadful warning of all that was to come. Five of the undergraduates of our year would be killed in action.

That night we ran our play well, and it was a beautiful evening. But Eliot's Te Deum seemed to me more profound than before.

Army

Alastair spent the summer vacation of 1939 working for the *Glasgow Herald*. In late August, with a declaration of war imminent, he was sent to fetch the editor, Sir William Robieson – who did not drive – back from his holiday retreat on Loch Fyne. He remained with the paper during the first weeks of the war, returning to Oxford for what was to be his last year at university.

In the summer of 1940 he failed his army medical due to inherited short sight. He had tried his best to pass the exam, memorising the letters on the board as he entered the room for the eye test, but was defeated by the observant doctor, who turned the card round the other way. He easily passed the rest of his medical, passing from one doctor to another, bit by bit, constantly having to deny that he was a Welshman, as they each remarked cheerfully on reading his papers: "We don't get many Welshmen up here!" The chairman of the board interviewed him at the end. "A lot of young lads," he said, "have failed the examination because of bad eyes. I'm afraid you won't be wanted for a long time, and perhaps not at all."

Although he had been rejected, he felt that he should be doing something more useful than returning to Oxford for his final year. The *Glasgow Herald* had lost so many of its journalists to the war that they were glad to take him on again, and he was glad to join them. That lasted for only a couple of months before he was called up in a non-combatant role as a private in the Pay Corps.

By coincidence, his cousin Alex Hetherington – five weeks

younger than Alastair and also short-sighted – was called up at the same time and both were posted to Perth. As their names differed by only one initial, they were billeted together, at first uncomfortably in a church and later in rather squalid lodgings near the South Inch, where there was no running water and the outside lavatory was shared among five families. They put forward a plea on their landlady's behalf and plumbing was soon installed, which improved matters all round.

Perth was a pleasant posting, though he found the work desperately dreary. The Pay Corps office was at Balhousie Castle, near the North Inch, and (typically) Alastair found he had just enough time to carry a sandwich lunch and climb to the top of Kinnoull Hill, with its fine views to the northern hills and over the widening estuary of the Tay, before the afternoon session at the castle. Every day there was an attempt to instil army drill into them for an hour, but many of the recruits were not particularly fit and their efforts in that direction were not of the best. Alastair himself, though very fit, was probably never what one might call a military man. (By the time we met in 1979 he had developed a slight "intellectual stoop" through sitting at his journalist's desk hour after hour; and his walk was casual, loose-limbed, rather than disciplined army style).

Perth boasted a repertory theatre with a weekly change of play, which Alastair enjoyed attending, whenever possible, as intermittent drama critic for the *Glasgow Herald*. The leading parts were mostly played by the resident quartet of Marjorie Dence, David Steuart (joint owners), with Valerie Lush and Wilfred Bentley: resident in the literal sense of the word, as almost the entire company lived together, in cramped and spartan quarters backstage. Despite these privations and a chronic shortage of money, Perth Theatre productions were remarkably good, as the *Herald's* critic frequently opined.

After a few months Alastair was promoted to lance corporal and posted back to Glasgow, working in the Mitchell Library and living comfortably at home once more in Principal's Lodgings. Work became more interesting too, as he was given the job of accompanying a major to take money to the naval ships waiting to leave the Clyde. They would drive down to Greenock or Gourock together and go on board assorted vessels waiting to sail, to deliver money-bags.

His enjoyment was marred by the discovery that many army families were suffering unnecessary hardship. These were wives whose husbands had been declared missing, but had not been recorded as officially dead. As a result they were receiving only one third of normal maintenance, leaving them in a financial plight, on top of personal misery. Many came to the office to plead that they were destitute, having to live on whatever friends and families could spare them. Despite official representations, it seemed that nothing was being done to help them.

At last Alastair decided to take matters into his own hands by writing privately to the Independent Liverpool MP Eleanor Rathbone, a family friend. Miss Rathbone, who was always prepared to take up cudgels on behalf of the underprivileged if their cause was just, made her own inquiries and raised the matter in parliament. Proper payment for the wives was quickly sanctioned. Questions were raised, however, as to how Miss Rathbone had received the information on which she had based her allegations. Although under some pressure, she did not reveal her source. Sir Hector disapproved of Alastair's tactics in leaking the story, though this was in no way due to lack of sympathy for the plight of the wives. Alastair was unrepentant, believing that whatever rules of ethics he might have broken, it had been in the best of causes. It was probably the only "leak" of his career.

In 1942 the Army's rules regarding eyesight were relaxed and Alastair was sent to the Royal Armoured Corps in Catterick for six weeks' training before going to OCTU Blackdown. After being commissioned he was attached to the 9th West Kent regiment, training cadets in Durham and Yorkshire, before transferring to the 2nd Northamptonshire Yeomanry, the armoured reconnaissance regiment of 11th Armoured Division. He privately thought the officers of his new regiment much less competent than those of 9th West Kent. ("They didn't know how to handle their tanks and never learned.")

While stationed at Aldershot, his father visited him, and together they went to Crondall in Hampshire to see an old friend of Sir Hector's. John Fowler Mitchell had been a friend and contemporary during Hector's student years at Glasgow University, and had been in the Indian Civil Service for many years. That reunion led to a meeting between Alastair and John's son Angus Mitchell, who later served with Alastair in the 11th Armoured Division, and who, with his wife Ann, became a life-long friend.

For many months the 2nd Northamptonshire Yeomanry trained and retrained over moorland and beaches, preparing for the awaited invasion of Europe. (Many years later, driving in Catalonia, Alastair accidentally grazed the side of a parked car. Distressed, he remarked to me that it was the first time he had ever done such a thing "except with a tank", and was surprised that I found this amusing.) When the invasion eventually came, 2nd Northamptonshire Yeomanry's arrival was substantially delayed owing to the weather, so it did not disembark in Normandy until June 17th. It disembarked from a landing ship on the beach at Courseulles, north-west of Caen, at midnight, in the middle of an air-raid, and parked its tanks under cover of a hedge. During the morning Alastair went for a walk and a scout round, passed a boarded-up restaurant, and knocked on the door. The proprietors, who had been sheltering from air raids in the cellar, were astonished, but eventually persuaded, and apparently pleased to be asked if they could provide dinner for a number of officers later that evening. A splendid meal was prepared, some hoarded Calavados produced: a strange beginning to what was to be a terrible experience for them all.

Alastair loathed fighting: shooting at other human beings intending to kill them. Although there were times that might almost be described as exhilaration during some battles, there were also times when he experienced fear. In that he was certainly not alone. After the war he avoided those memories – of the hideous wounds and deaths of friends, the noise and smell of carnage – and rarely spoke of it.

The regiment's first real action was at the village of Haut du Bosq, by the River Odon, on June 26th. By the 30th it had lost a lot of men and tanks and was withdrawn to reorganise.

During July it was sent to support infantry round Rauray, keeping under cover, and crossed the River Orne overnight on July 17th. That was the eve of the operation known as

Goodwood, with its appalling loss of life. Alastair recalled its beginning:

> At 7am next morning the sky was superbly clear and we watched a 1000-bomber raid taking place as we moved towards a hill about half a mile from the German forward line. Bombers came streaming in from the sea and were actually releasing their bombs straight above us at times. The concussion was tremendous – one's ear drums banged in and out – and the gap made in the enemy defences appeared as a dust wall, dense, dark brown, rising several hundred feet into the air (or so it seemed). That evening I watched German tanks up by Bras trying to pick off some of ours, about 200 yards from where I was standing.

Fierce fighting with many losses continued throughout July. At one point during a battle Alastair was sent off to reconnoitre, and he walked out along a railway embankment to get a better view. Strangely, at an Army conference held at Aldershot long after the war (about 1952), some German officers present remembered that incident. They had been hidden in a bunker beside the railway line and had kept Alastair in the sights of their guns, but did not fire for fear of indicating their own presence.

On August 1st the whole division passed down a track through l'Eveque forest (an unguarded boundary between two German divisions) leading to an intact bridge over the Souleuvre river five miles behind the German lines – a lucky breakthrough – and pushed on into le Beny Bocage; on the 3rd, Alastair's tank was blown up and one of his crew killed, two others wounded. (He found the tank shortly after the end of the war, still parked beside a hedge in an orchard). Most of the squadron were lost then. Alastair had been wounded: a bullet had gone through the flesh of his upper arm and out the other side, quite painlessly (it had been his sergeant who pointed it out as the blood dripped down his sleeve and hand), though it took ten years for the hole to disappear completely. He was sent back, slept for twenty four hours, and returned on the night of August 4th.

On August 14 we attacked again, this time for Estry, and got about four miles southwards. The great Normandy sack was then forming, and the Americans were said to be getting near Argentan from the south. We had a most uncomfortable afternoon and night close to a village called Thiel, since the Germans were shooting off all their remaining shells preparatory to withdrawing.

Of the sixty officers of the 2nd Northamptonshire Yeomanry, only nineteen were now left and the regiment was broken up. At that point Alastair was asked to become an intelligence officer with the 11th Armoured Division. His instructions were to be in the forefront of all that was happening and to report back to Major General "Pip" Roberts, its commander.

About 7.30 or 8am on the morning of the August 30, I was following closely behind the first tanks advancing into Amiens in a scout car, with driver. We had driven all night through heavy rain, which ceased about 4am. I believe that the commander of Panzer Group West, General Hans Eberbach, had spent the night at his HQ in Amiens (I have a recollection of a rather beautiful large house), quite unaware of the British advance. He believed that we were still at least thirty miles away, and set off from his HQ that morning on an inspection of his own lines, accompanied by an officer – an adjutant, perhaps. His staff car was preceded by another German vehicle. They had just turned into the road out of their HQ when the leading vehicle ran into the British advance and was shot at. One of its occupants was killed outright, and two were badly wounded.
I came on this scene five or six minutes later. Our men were surrounding both vehicles and their occupants, some attending the wounded. I stopped my scout car and waited beside them. Word had been sent to General Horrocks, Commander 30 Corps, who arrived about twenty minutes later. He decided not to speak to Eberbach himself, and ordered the advance to continue without further delay. He instructed the senior officer present to have Eberbach taken to Montgomery's HQ, and I was ordered to do it.

We all piled into my scout car. Eberbach sat in front beside the driver, while his adjutant (if that is who it was) sat in the back with me. I held my gun directed at the general, and we drove about fifty miles back through our own lines. Our people, heading for Amiens, were amazed to see us driving towards them with what was obviously an important captive. Their initial reaction was first of curiosity, followed by astonishment, and finally, as we passed them, and they could see that a German general had been taken prisoner, of high excitement.

Eberbach's reactions were also of astonishment. He simply could not believe what he was seeing. Every few minutes he gasped and shook his head at the scale and speed of the British advance. He had set out from his HQ in the belief that his troops were still firmly entrenched for many miles round the city.

We reached Montgomery's HQ and I spoke to the guards, asking them to pass on the news of our arrival. They suggested that they would guard the scout car while I went to inform Monty's staff. Montgomery decided that he did not wish to interview Eberbach personally. We were instructed to deliver him to a camp about three miles away, where other captured German officers were being held.

As we approached the camp perimeter we could see a large number – probably 130 or 140 – of German officers sitting on the grass. As the gates opened to let us in and they could see who was arriving, they immediately rose to their feet, forming a shocked and silent semi-circle. Eberbach approached them and walked slowly round the group, shaking each officer by the hand. It was an impressive moment. I believe Eberbach was flown back to London that afternoon. I quickly caught up with the advance again as we sped through France, towards the Belgium frontier.

Alastair's greatest wartime adventure (shared with all 11th Armoured Division) was still to come, and he recounted it in the *Guardian* fifty years later. (See page 141.)

As the war dragged to an end, the 11th Armoured moved on, spending the winter camped uncomfortably in Holland. But by March they had begun to move east, into Germany, towards the advancing Russians, and VE Day in May found them near Lubeck, almost at the point of contact with them. A few days after the German surrender had been signed, Alastair was sent, with his OC, to accept formal surrender by the North Friesian Islands. They toured the islands by speedboat, and at each one they were taken ashore in an ancient horse-drawn cart that came across the sands at low tide to meet them. They were courteously greeted by each island mayor, who prefaced his welcome by declaring how profoundly he had disagreed with the Nazi regime. At the request of the War Office Alastair mapped the coastline, before returning to Division HQ at Plon Castle in Schleswig-Holstein's lake district.

From September 1945 until his demobilisation the following year, Alastair was posted to Hamburg to begin – as editorial controller – the setting up of a new, politically-free newspaper, *Die Welt*, covering the British zone. He had learned German before going to Normandy, so was fairly fluent. Theoretically he could have been released from the army to return to Oxford, as many of his contemporaries were doing. But Alastair was impatient to get on with his life. Running *Die Welt* for a while was to be a splendid experience, and he learned a great deal very quickly.

Hamburg had been largely destroyed, but they found a building from which a Nazi newspaper had been published, and were able to use their old equipment. Alastair appointed a staff of about twelve German journalists who were known, beyond a shadow of a doubt, to have been opposed to the Nazis. From their own newspaper experience they knew exactly how to go about things, and the paper was soon up and running.

The chief amongst these, Küstermeier, who became editor, had been imprisoned and tortured by the Nazis; as a result he could work for only a few hours each day, but he understood exactly what was needed. Alastair thought he was a marvellous man, who, despite poor and ever-declining health, was determined to do all that he could to see the paper well established.

Alastair read everything himself before it went to print, though he was confident there was no real need for it. He would arrive at the office about 10am and rarely returned home until after midnight. He was nominally under the command of a Colonel Garland, who was perfectly happy to leave everything to Alastair. Garland was a delightful and courteous man, later a professor at Exeter. He would ride to the office on horseback, at about 11am, believing that such a sight demonstrated a proper example of Britishness. The German police always stopped the traffic to allow him to pass. On arrival he would make a few inquiries and depart on horseback shortly afterwards.

Die Welt went out overnight on five days a week. The Germans had been starved of honest, impartial journalism since 1933 and they bought the paper eagerly. Because of shortages, the number of copies was limited and they were always snapped up by 9am.

One of the important members of staff was Ilse Kramann, Alastair's personal assistant. Before the war, as a young girl, she had lived in South Africa, but the family had been compulsorily repatriated to Germany in 1944. When Alastair left the army, and the paper, in the autumn of 1946, to return to Scotland, Ilse went to work in Berlin – still employed by *Die Welt* – where she somehow managed to upset the Russian authorities seriously. They captured, imprisoned, and tortured her for nine months and sentenced her to internment for twenty five years in a slave camp in the Arctic: I think it was Vorkuta. There she froze, starved, and hauled heavy timber from lorries, day after day without hope or respite.

Five years later, Adenauer made a deal with the Russians which allowed her and many others to return to Germany. She eventually reached South Africa, married a childhood friend, Manfred Fleischmann, and later emigrated to run a sheep farm with him in western Canada.

In the spring of 1996, having been out of touch with Alastair for fifty years, Ilse traced his address, and she and Manfred came to stay with us, and to explore Scotland. She was a tiny, sweet, soft-spoken woman, delighted to have renewed their old friendship at last. On several occasions during her visit she spoke sadly of the shortness of life. After returning home Isle became ill and died the following summer.

In August 1946 Alastair was decommissioned from the army and returned home to resume work at the *Glasgow Herald*. He was almost twenty-seven and more than ready to begin his career in journalism in earnest.

Glasgow Herald
as recalled by Alastair himself

The aroma at the Mitchell Street entrance – then the side in the lane – remains most vivid among early memories. It was a melding of hot oil from the machine room, newsprint from the stacks, and ink: it spoke of newspapers, of sweaty engineering, and of the excitement of going to press. Years later, shortly before the *Herald* left Mitchell Street, I was in the building and the aroma was still there, if mildly muted by antiseptic. To a young journalist it was a daily stimulus.

Andy Anderson, the chief sub-editor, was another daily stimulation – as indeed, in a quieter way, was the editor, Bill Robieson (Sir William). Andy Anderson had a news sense as sharply refined as any I have ever encountered, and I learned probably more from him than from any other single journalist (apart later from A.P. Wadsworth at the *Guardian*).

He occasionally beat his desk with his big metal column rule in apparent ferocity, and his words could be tart. But he helped a trainee to learn fast, through encouragement and criticism and by his own enthusiasm.

My first days in the *Herald* were in the sub-editors' room, from May to August 1940 and again when I returned from the Army in 1946. Bill Robieson believed that as a starting point the subs' provided better discipline and a broader view than the reporters' room, a view no longer widely shared. It gave me a good grounding, though I was happy in 1947 to be moved for a time to reporting in London (with a bit of subbing still thrown in, especially at weekends).

Robieson also sent me to Germany for a time the following summer, when Berlin was first blockaded. That, too, was an opportunity. But I suppose that the most persistent influence on me of Robieson's editorship was through his daily meeting with leader writers in which I took part for two years before moving to the *Guardian* in Manchester in 1950. It seemed a leisurely exchange in mid-afternoon. It was his habit to discuss the stories that should be followed up, and allocate them in a quite arbitrary way to those (usually five) of us who were present. Thus – to our great benefit – we all became used to tackling anything and everything. I can only remember one occasion when a member of the leader-writing team, instructed to follow up a particular story, refused point blank, announced that he had "no intention of doing anything about that", and abruptly left the building for the day. Robieson gave no hint that he was taken aback. He merely looked at the rest of us and remarked imperturbably, "Oh well, no doubt one of you will do it". As far as I am aware, no subsequent sanctions were taken. Robieson was not a man to hold a grudge.

If I wanted an extra day away among the mountains, Andy Anderson was willing to let me have it, so long as I made up for it in an earlier or later week. For better or worse, for a time in 1947 and early '48 – on Fridays, but only on Fridays – I was left in charge of the newsroom from midnight or soon after, until 3.15 or 3.30am, when work ended. That had an advantage. In spring and summer, if the weather looked like being good, I dozed in a comfortable chair (one of lamentably few) in the office until it was time to catch the 6 am train to Fairlie, where I got the 7.15 (I think) boat to Brodick. Having breakfasted on board, I could be on my way to Goatfell or Cir Mhor by 8.20 or thereabouts, with a weekend's enjoyable climbing ahead.

It was one of those Saturday mornings in 1947 that years later gave me the opening words of a book: "What's news?" It was a beautiful day, and leaning over the rails of the Arran ferry just after 7am, I watched the morning's newspapers being slid down an open ramp into the boat. By accident the man on the pier slid the load to one side and it dropped into the water. Among the papers sinking into the Clyde was the *Glasgow Herald,* on which I had worked all night.

"Awa' and get a hook, Willie," called the man on the boat to the one on the pier.

"Ach, no, it's no worth it", said Willie. "It's all lies and trash anyway".

A few moments later, he relented and went fishing with a strong hook. Three good bags were saved.

Manchester Guardian

By 1950 Alastair had been back at the *Glasgow Herald* for almost four years, and he began to feel that it was time to widen his experience. He arranged to call on A.P. Wadsworth, editor of the *Manchester Guardian*, on a free day, to discuss the possibilities for the future in general. They had a friendly talk, but nothing specific was mentioned, so he was surprised when Wadsworth rang Robieson a week or two later to say that, with Robieson's consent, he would like Alastair to join the paper as defence correspondent.

Robieson was genuinely disappointed to learn that Alastair was leaving, but he was charming, remarking that he was indeed fortunate to be going to the *Manchester Guardian* to work under Wadsworth, whom he admired. He generously wished Alastair all the best.

Alastair went to live in pleasant rooms in a family home in Didsbury – the largely Victorian area to the south of the city – which A.P. Wadsworth had found for him, a few minutes' walk from his own home. Wadsworth found this useful, as he was able to invite Alastair round for discussions frequently. Alastair loved "Waddy", describing him as a marvellous man and a wonderful editor.

At the time of AP's retirement through ill-health in 1956, Alastair wrote a long leader about him, which began:

> There have been nights when Mr Wadsworth wrote nearly all the leaders himself, kept a close watch on the news columns, and handled a large correspondence. He takes the work of three or four men in his stride. Even during the past few months, when unhappily he has not been able to leave home, the flow of advice and leading articles has been kept up. APW has an uncanny knack of grasping instantly the vital implications of a complex event, and he can put his thoughts on paper with greater speed and clarity than anyone I have ever known.

Alastair walked the few miles to and from the office each day for exercise, a custom that amused or bemused some of his new colleagues. At first he was home-sick for his beloved hills and for the companionship of old friends in Glasgow. He was grateful, though, to Paddy Monkhouse, the deputy editor, who took the time and trouble to introduce him to the Peak District, in compensation for weekends formerly spent on Lomond, Vorlich, the Cobbler. Others on the staff were equally friendly, and the *Manchester Guardian* was a joy to work for. If he had accepted his parents' and grandparents' advice to have a specific goal in life, Alastair had surely attained that goal now.

In his speech at the *Guardian's* 150th birthday celebrations in 1971, Alastair reflected on those first months:

> When I joined the *Guardian* in Manchester twenty one years ago, there were no telephones either in the editorial "corridor" or in the reporters' room. This was not because the *Guardian* scorned modern machinery: at that time its technical director was developing the most advanced form of facsimile transmission in the world. It was because the people who edited the paper cared about other virtues: rational thought, good writing, and the peace to concentrate. If you were wanted on the telephone, a messenger asked you to take the call in one of the booths off the reporters' room or at the end of the "corridor". And if you were at work writing, you could politely decline. The atmosphere of the office was that of a senior common room: collegiate, thoughtful, friendly and at once both intensely serious and cheerfully irreverent.

Two years after his arrival in Manchester, Alastair was awarded a Commonwealth scholarship to spend a year in America, mostly studying at Princeton. Although he was comparatively new to the staff, Wadsworth encouraged him to grasp the opportunity and take an unpaid year off, believing it to be in the paper's interests for Alastair to spend some time in the States. He enthusiastically advised Alastair where to go, what to avoid, and what not to miss on any account.

Alastair had glimpsed Alistair Cooke (already something of a legend) in 1951, when he came from America during the British general election. Cooke had gone to Lancashire with Wadsworth. As it happened Alastair was asked to go and cover a meeting in the same area, and they passed in their cars. Alastair had a vivid recollection of both Wadsworth and Cooke giving him a great wave, and of being surprised and delighted by the warmth of it.

He sailed for New York in early September 1952, paying for his passage by giving lectures to the passengers, though the weather was atrocious throughout the voyage and his audiences were small. The ship arrived two days late because of the storms. To his surprise, Cooke came to see him at once, and was friendly, jolly, welcoming, full of sound advice, and invited Alastair to stay with his wife Jane and himself at their apartment overlooking Central Park. Alastair stayed with them for about a week, finding his way round the city, taking the compulsory driving test, and so forth. He found their kindness and generosity amazing and their advice invaluable.

A few days later he parked his belongings at Nassau Hall, Princeton, bought a car, and drove westwards on his first journey of exploration. Somewhere, in a beautiful house about half-way between New York and Washington, he had a dinner engagement with a friend of his father's. General Eisenhower was one of the other guests. Until recently supreme commander of NATO, Eisenhower was now Republican candidate in the forthcoming presidential election. His Democratic opponent was Adlai Stevenson, the intellectual governor of Illinois.

Discovering that Alastair was on the staff of the *Manchester Guardian*, Eisenhower immediately asked their host if they might go somewhere private before dinner so that they could talk, and they were ushered to the library. Eisenhower was much exercised by the British opinion polls, which were showing Stevenson in the lead, and he wanted an explanation. Alastair was conscious (though he thought Eisenhower probably was not) that he had written a critical leader on the general's recent campaigning style a few weeks earlier, commenting that he seemed to be a new character – "not the prudent general, nor the candidate as we have known him so far, but Saint Ike, crusader against the Communist dragon and liberator of the captive peoples. It is a change from the cautious and well-chosen way of speech he had in Europe....Simply to talk of liberation, as Mr Eisenhower has done, is to warrant condemnation for the very thing he attacks in the present Administration – loud policies and faint deeds...."

The reason for the almost universal assumption on both sides of the Atlantic that Stevenson would inherit the mantle of Roosevelt and Truman was largely because it seemed odds-on that the twenty-year supremacy of the Democrats would continue – and besides, Stevenson was an experienced, if rather obscure, politician, whereas Eisenhower had no political background.

Eisenhower believed that reports of the British polls were damaging to his campaign, and he seemed dismayed and rather affronted that British opinion should now be against him, after the public acclaim and honour he had always received there. Alastair was aware of his blue eyes appraising him as they spoke, and his mind went back to his own days as a humble young intelligence officer during the Allied invasion of France. Now the overlord of that great victory was sitting beside him, seeking his advice: the situation seemed unreal. (He would later also meet Montgomery in not dissimilar circumstances.) He assured the general that no personal slight was intended, that British people were fond of betting on such matters, and that in any case opinion polls often turned out to be wrong. By the end of the half-hour conversation Eisenhower seemed mollified, if still slightly perplexed: and a few weeks later he went on to confound the forecasters – American and British – by achieving a personal triumph at the election.

At the end of October Alastair returned to Princeton, where he began a short, but intensive, study of American politics under the aegis of George Graham, professor of politics. A fellow student was John P. Mackintosh, later a professor of politics in Scotland, later still MP for East Lothian, whose early death – like those of Alick Buchanan-Smith and of John Smith in later years – was a great loss to Scottish politics. Princeton was a forty-five minute train ride from New York, and Alastair saw the Cookes quite often. Alistair was already broadcasting his regular *Letter from America*, and Alastair had also been asked to do a regular fifteen-minute broadcast for the BBC. (A much lower-profile affair altogether, he said.) It suited the BBC for them to make their broadcasts on the same day, at the same time – usually on a Thursday, about mid-day. Alastair broadcast for fifteen minutes. One minute before he ended, Cooke would slip into the seat beside him, ready to take over the microphone for his own broadcast, while Alastair remained seated beside him.

Alastair noted the contrast between their styles. He had written out his talk, rehearsed it several times, timed it exactly, and approached the microphone nervously. Alistair came in nonchalantly, with a few notes and a small piece of paper, and he began to speak off the cuff in his elegant way. He always knew exactly what he was going to say, but he would gently meander up and down fascinating highways and byways of history and memory before rounding up the theme of the talk with his final punch-line exactly on time. "It was always a tour de force and I sat and listened in admiration."

Another acquaintance of his father's, Albert Einstein, lived about fifteen minutes' walk from Alastair's room at Princeton, and Alastair was invited over to tea with him almost every week. Einstein seemed to Alastair – then aged about thirty-two – to be a very old man, but he always found him in excellent humour and a rather jolly host. His recollection was that Einstein made and dispensed tea himself. Einstein kindly refrained from discussing matters of science, but seemed genuinely interested in Alastair's political studies and constantly challenged his guest's reasons for taking a particular line, causing him to think and re-think everything through very carefully before arriving at a conclusion: scientific methodology applied to journalism. It was a lesson that Alastair did not forget.

In February he headed west in his car, beginning by visiting Washington, where he had his first encounter with Max Freedman, Washington correspondent for the *Manchester Guardian*. He described Max as a single-minded, hard-working and devoted journalist, a Canadian from Winnipeg, who knew everyone and everything that was happening in political circles in Washington. (Throughout his editorship Freedman plied him with amazing background briefings emanating from the highest sources in Washington – including the president(s) – sometimes marked "Totally, totally, totally off the record". These ranged from pre-knowledge of Britain's plans for the Suez operation, background to the Cuban crisis, the Kennedy view prior to Vietnam, and details of a curious row between Kennedy and Diefenbaker of Canada, who had apparently treated Kennedy abominably.)

On Max's recommendation Alastair went up to visit Montreal and Ottawa before embarking on a solo car journey that would take him – with many stops – through Minnesota, South Dakota, Wyoming, Colorado, Utah, and Nevada. In his capacity as defence correspondent he was invited to visit Camp Roberts to see part of the American army in training for Korea – though here the desert heat proved too much for him and he was rushed to hospital to recover.

Denis Brogan – by now professor of political science at Cambridge – was then in California, researching his seminal book on American politics, and Alastair enjoyed meeting his old tutor now on more or less equal terms. For his part Brogan must have been gratified that his pre-war efforts at Corpus had borne fruit. Alastair stayed in San Francisco for several days – a beautiful city which he would have enjoyed more but for the fact that he was in severe pain and had to have two badly abscessed teeth removed. Things improved a great deal when Alistair Cooke flew over from New York and showed him round the city, between high-level engagements of his own. By now it was almost July, and the drive took him up the west coast to Portland, Oregon, in the company of Jules Mencken, as far as Seattle and Spokane, before heading off eastwards again via Montana, Wyoming, Colorado, Kansas, Missouri, Illinois, Indiana, Ohio, and Pennsylvania. Those impressions of America – particularly of amazing days spent climbing in the Rockies and walking in the Grand Canyon – were never to be forgotten.

He returned to the Clyde by Cunarder in early August and was back at work in Manchester towards the end of the month. Now, in addition to being the *Manchester Guardian's* defence correspondent, he was appointed the paper's foreign editor. An offer from Roy Thomson in 1954 to become editor of *the Scotsman* was gracefully refused: as far as Alastair was concerned, there could be no contest. He was more than content with his life. But it was about to change yet again. A.P. Wadsworth had kept the knowledge of his illness within his family circle for as long as possible, but by the summer of 1956 the gravity of his condition became more generally known and the senior staff learned, to their sorrow, that Waddy was dying.

To Alastair's astonishment (but with Wadsworth's knowledge and approval) he was informed by the chairman, Laurence Scott, that he was to be appointed to succeed APW as editor, though he was asked to keep the news to himself for a month: which he was glad to be able to do, as it gave him a chance to recover from the shock. Alastair acknowledged that he might not have been the first choice of all the staff, for a number of reasons: he was only thirty-six, newish to the paper, Scottish rather than Mancunian. He was also perhaps viewed as a little austere, shy and straight-laced in manner. Some – perhaps many – would have expected that the older and more experienced deputy editor, Paddy Monkhouse, would have been chosen. Any initial dismay was quickly swallowed, however, and they – Paddy probably most of all – rallied round their new editor. Alastair felt at once that he had their loyalty and trust – which was merciful, for he had what he himself described as a "fiery baptism"...

Sources

Throughout: Alastair's letters, diaries and conversations; personal research.

Sir Charles Illingworth's book on Sir Hector, *University Statesman* (George Outram, 1971).

Recollections of Alistair Cooke are based on an interview between Alastair and Nick Clarke.

I am grateful to Dr Angus Mitchell, CB, CVO, MC and to Brigadier E.R. Holmes, OBE, TD, Ministry of Defence, for help with the account of Alastair's Normandy experiences, which I based on letters to his father and on my own conversations with him.

Many thanks to Kenneth Roy for editing my lengthy text. – S.H.

A great editor

John Grigg

Alastair Hetherington will go down in history as one of the great British editors of the twentieth century. Under his leadership a provincial newspaper with a national reputation became national in the full sense, shedding the "Manchester" from its title, moving to London – first for printing, then for editing – and becoming the sole British national broadsheet of the left. Appointed editor at the relatively early age of thirty-six, he was not quite so young as his illustrious predecessor C.P. Scott, who started his long reign (1872-1929) at the age of twenty-five. But then Alastair did not have the advantage of being a cousin of the proprietor. His period as editor, though much shorter than Scott's (just under twenty years, compared with nearly sixty), was nevertheless quite long by modern standards; and in some ways it was even more remarkable. As well as upholding the Scott tradition of editorial robustness and independence, Alastair played a vital part in preserving the *Guardian's* identity, when it was threatened with death by merger.

No editor that I can think of has faced a more searching test of his or her qualities at the very moment of assuming office. Alastair effectively took over from the dying A.P. Wadsworth on October 17, 1956, as the so-called Suez crisis was reaching its climax. The British and French governments were, at the time, planning their attack on Egypt, in collusion with Israel. A fortnight later they used Israel's invasion of Sinai and advance to the Suez Canal as a pretext for an ultimatum to both parties, demanding withdrawal from the Canal. When, naturally enough, this was rejected by Egypt, British and French forces were sent in, ostensibly to "separate the combatants".

Alastair's reaction to the Anglo-French ultimatum was uniquely prompt and unequivocal. While other papers that might have been expected to condemn the government's action without delay, such as the *Daily Mirror*, the *Daily Herald* and the *News Chronicle*, hesitated for forty-eight hours, and even the labour leadership in Parliament did so for twenty-four, Alastair wrote a leader for the following day's paper in which he described the ultimatum as "an act of folly, without justification in any terms but brief expediency". There was nothing sloppy about his attitude. He was as good a patriot as anyone, recognising legitimate national interests and the need to defend them. Though not remotely a warmonger, he was equally remote from pacifism. His opposition to Suez was thoroughly realistic, as well as principled.

It was also entirely consistent with the line he had been taking since the beginning of the crisis. Already, as foreign and defence editor, he was bound to have a very considerable influence on the policy of the paper, and Wadsworth's enfeebled state made his role all the greater during the period immediately before he succeeded as editor. On August 2, a few days after Nasser's announcement that the Suez Canal Company would be nationalised, he had written a leader which set the *Guardian* on a firm course. The government, he said, was right to prepare for military action, but should resort to it only if Nasser were to close the Canal. His leader in response to the ultimatum, and his utter condemnation of the subsequent attack on Egypt, were logically in line with his initial assessment.

Nobody could accuse him of acting from motives of "brief expediency". In the short term the new editor's strong-mindedness and courage cost the paper thousands of readers (eight or nine thousand in the Manchester area alone). And two big companies cancelled their advertising in the paper. But as events vindicated Alastair's policy he was deservedly rewarded by a marked net growth in circulation. At the beginning of the crisis it stood at 165,000; by the end, about 30,000 had been lost, but about 46,000 had been gained. There were to be ups and downs in the future, largely due to economic circumstances, but politically the *Guardian* strengthened its position permanently as a result of Alastair's anti-Suez stand.

He was supported in it throughout by the company chairman, Laurence Scott, a grandson of C.P. It was therefore all the more painful and difficult for Alastair to find himself, later, in opposition to Scott, when the chairman was seeking a merger between the *Guardian* and the *Times*. The reasoning behind this proposal was primarily economic; both papers were losing money, and seemed likely to go under if they persisted in the attempt to exist independently. The idea of a merger was raised by Scott in November 1965, and finally abandoned a year later. During the months when it was under discussion the matter absorbed a large amount of Alastair's time, causing him much anxiety and distracting him from the anyway full-time job of editing the paper. But in the end the identity and independence of the *Guardian* were saved, without prejudice to its economic viability. He deserves much of the credit for this happy outcome, though he would be the first to acknowledge the decisive contribution of Richard Scott (Laurence's cousin), who was chairman of the Scott Trust (as distinct from the company).

My own acquaintance with Alastair began at the time of the Suez crisis, on which our views emphatically coincided. In 1960 he asked me to write a regular column for the *Guardian*, which I did weekly, and for a time twice-weekly, over the next nine years. We became close friends, and when he and Miranda moved to London in the mid-1960s we also became close neighbours in the Blackheath area. We would often go for walks together in Greenwich Park, and during the prolonged merger crisis Alastair took me into his confidence about the course of negotiations. (William Haley, editor of the *Times*, was an even closer neighbour, but I never discussed the affair with him, though we were on excellent terms). Alastair no doubt felt free to confide in me, because he knew that I was on his side but otherwise not involved. I was an outside contributor to the paper, not a member of the *Guardian* staff.

His choice of me as a columnist shows how broad-minded he was as editor. At the time I was a Conservative, if of a heterodox kind, and what I wrote often conflicted with his own opinions and the opinions of the paper. But he gave me absolute freedom, subject only to warning me occasionally if he felt that I was devoting too much attention to a particular subject. He used to say – indeed he has said in print (in *Guardian Years*) – that he felt my columns were of value to the paper because of their "range and originality". I quote this flattering comment mainly to show that he wanted the paper to reflect a wide variety of views and to challenge the assumptions of its traditional readers. A strong line was laid down in editorials, but he did not expect all opinions expressed in the paper to conform to it. On the contrary, he welcomed and encouraged controversy.

On many issues, of course, we tended to agree, and we also agreed about many public personalities. For instance, we were both pro-Europe, and Jo Grimond was a politician we were both fond of and admired. I could not, however, share Alastair's good opinion of Harold Wilson as leader of the opposition or as prime minister. Very often I felt moved to attack Wilson, and granted his almost paranoid reaction to press criticism it must have been embarrassing for Alastair to have a columnist writing about him as I did. But there was never the slightest question of censorship. If Alastair had any trouble with Wilson on my account, he must have felt that it was a price worth paying for the manifest freedom of the paper and its contributors. In time Alastair became disillusioned with Wilson himself, but meanwhile he never allowed his personal partiality to lead him into making the *Guardian* an organ of Wilsonian propaganda.

I have mentioned our walks in Greenwich Park. We also sometimes walked together in Scotland. On one occasion he led my wife and me on a walk from the west end of Loch Affric through to the West Coast, a distance of about twenty seven miles. This seemed a long enough walk to us, but to him it was little more than a stroll, if only because it was mainly on the flat. His idea of serious walking is to climb as many mountains as daylight permits.

He has always seemed most at home in Scotland, and is certainly the most quintessential Scot I have ever known. But there is a bit of a paradox here – or anyway an apparent paradox – which may contain a lesson for our times. Alastair was born in Wales, and largely educated in England. Above all, the most important part of his working life was spent in England, and his name will forever be associated with a great newspaper that is basically English. Like his father, Sir Hector – an eminent academic and university administrator – he has remained a true Scot, in accent and (more significantly) in spirit, while deploying his talents within the wider British community. But when he left the *Guardian* he returned to work in Scotland, and it is in Scotland that he now lives in retirement, with Sheila. He is as far from being a renegade as from being a Scottish chauvinist. His motto might be, "What should they know of Scotland who only Scotland know?"

Those fellow Scots who are intent on breaking the Union are, like him, proudly conscious of Scotland's identity as a nation, and rightly so. Few nations that are also nation-states – with flags, ambassadors, air lines, and all the other paraphernalia of statehood – have anything like the national character that Scotland is universally seen to have. (Many of them have no national character at all.) But it is surely true that most of the events, personalities and traits that have contributed to Scotland's extraordinarily high profile as a nation date from the time since, rather than before, the Act of Union. The two Scots who have done most to define Scotland's identity in the eyes of the world – Robert Burns and Sir Walter Scott – were both post-Union men. And the most fruitful period in the whole history of Scotland, comparable with the great age of Athens, the Italian Renaissance, or the Elizabethan age in England, was the period of the Scottish Enlightenment at the end of the eighteenth century.

If either of the two nations that joined to form Great Britain has suffered a loss of identity, it is England rather than Scotland. Moreover, the power and influence exercised by Scots both within the Union and (while it lasted) the British empire have been out of all proportion to their numbers. Seven of the United Kingdom's twenty prime ministers this century have been native Scots or Scots of the diaspora, and in every other department of UK life Scots have been notably dominant.

Perhaps the most important of all British institutions to come into being during the present century, the BBC, was the more or less single-handed creation of a Scot, John Reith. He provided both its structure and its ethos, with profound consequences for British society. But many other scarcely less potent Scottish figures could be mentioned in our twentieth century roll of honour. Alastair is one of them.

As I write, the United Kingdom has the most Scottish government it has ever experienced, while at the same time Scotland (though not England) is receiving a devolved government of its own, together with continued over-representation at Westminster and a heavy subsidy at the expense of English taxpayers. Scottish Raj is the order of the day. I pray that there will be no English backlash, because it would be a sad day if the likes of Alastair were to be forced to choose between emigration and a career restricted geographically and culturally.

I say "the likes of Alastair", but of course there is nobody quite like him. That is why we are all contributing to this book.

Are you sober?

Anthony Howard

My first indirect encounter with the then editor of the *Manchester Guardian*, who had been in office for just two years, was not exactly propitious. On the strength (or weakness) of some cuttings I had submitted, I had been invited to Manchester for an interview to see whether, at the age of twenty-four, I had the makings of a suitable recruit for the famous Cross Street reporters' room. When I arrived, I was greeted by Harry Whewell, the news editor, who – sitting at a rolltop desk almost straight out of Ben Hecht's *The Front Page* – genially explained that the editor had been called away "on pressing business" and that, therefore, the most I could expect that day was a sort of preliminary, exploratory chat with him. Our talk seemed to go well enough – Harry even bought me a lunchtime pint at the office hostelry, Rowntree's, round the back of the Cross Street building – but when we returned to the news room to collect my coat Harry rummaged in his desk to produce the dog-eared clippings I had sent in and handed them back to me.

It was only on the train returning to London that I opened the envelope up. Attached to the juvenalia I had nervously presented was a little note signed "AH" – the editor's initials as well as mine. It started off with the brisk announcement that on the day I was due to arrive he expected to be "over the hills and far away" climbing in the Lake District – but that this didn't really matter as he hadn't much cared for "the supercilious tone" of my writing. Would Harry anyway go through the motions of talking to me – and then, when he got back, he would write me a formal note saying in effect "Thanks, but no thanks"? Ploughing my way back to Euston – the train journey in those days took almost four and a half hours – I felt a bit crestfallen. Plainly, fate had deemed that I was never to be allowed to follow in the footsteps of such legendary figures as Howard Spring or Neville Cardus. Harry, though, must have done his best for me – for within a week I received not the anticipated brush-off but an invitation to go and talk to Alastair Hetherington in the *Manchester Guardian's* London office, which in those days was just above the Post Office in Fleet Street and virtually next-door to El Vino.

This time, however, there was no offer of a friendly drink – just a fresh-faced, fair-haired figure sitting behind an immaculately tidy desk as he conducted a predominantly businesslike interview. At the end of it, he said (with I thought just a touch of trepidation) that – if the idea still appealed to me – I could join the *MG* in Manchester for a trial period of three months starting on January 1, 1959, at a salary of £20 a week.

It was £10 a week less than I was then getting from the long-since defunct Co-operative Sunday newspaper *Reynolds News.* But I accepted with alacrity – and have never regretted it. Within a month I had been summoned to Manchester again – this time to spend my day off (Monday) getting to know the "feel" of the office and to stay the night at the editor's home in Didsbury Park. That is not the kind of thing, I fancy, that would happen with editors today – but those were far more informal days and, in any event, Alastair, in his frugal way, saw to it that I sang for my bed and board by actually composing a leader (about the new Labour shadow cabinet) on the very first evening I ever passed in Cross Street.

Taking the leader (knocked out on an antediluvian typewriter in the reporters' room) into him in his office on "the corridor" was, I suppose, one of the more intimidating experiences of my early journalistic life – not helped by his very first question to me being "Are you sober?" (I had meanwhile, in an effort to boost my confidence, that evening been back to Rowntree's.) I sat across the desk from him trying not to breathe beer fumes over him, as with a sharp pencil he deleted a sentence here or there, added a phrase somewhere else and then finally changed my rousing concluding sentence from a statement into a question. He then threw the ms back at me and inquired whether his changes and emendations were okay by me. They were far more than "okay": they had transformed my essentially amateur effort into a professional piece of work. It was my first lesson in one of the necessary attributes of an editor. Whatever else he may be, he should always possess the gift of being the alchemist of other people's copy.

Alastair had that talent in abundance – and for the next eighteen months I was to be the beneficiary of it. The *MG* in those days was not even printing in London, and the offices in Cross Street resembled in many ways an old curiosity shop. There was, for example, on the editor's desk a rubber stamp and a pad of violet ink in a tin. The stamp bore the letters "AH" and, once they had been imprinted on any piece of copy, it meant that the "subs" interfered with it only at their peril. Since Alastair – whether out of motives of protectiveness or simple prudence – insisted that all my copy went direct to him, I was the recipient almost from the day I started in Manchester of distinctly "favoured nation" treatment. I do not think at the time I had the slightest notion of how lucky I was: that realisation came only later, when I spent an unhappy year working at the Thomson *Sunday Times* as the victim of tough old brutes on the subs' table who viewed their task as one of turning the idiosyncratic loaves that reporters delivered into processed bread.

But there was a downside, of course, to being brought so closely under the editor's wing. If one made mistakes, they were not forgotten or forgiven. Six years after he ceased to be editor, Alastair was still ruefully to recall in his memoirs – *Guardian Years* (1981) – what he termed "the one bad lapse" in the paper's coverage of the 1959 election campaign. It was something he characterised as "an unbalanced, late edition report" of Harold Macmillan's final rally at Bellevue, Manchester, a few days before polling day. The heading on that front-page sketch – "Full stomachs in faithful congregation" – was not mine but the copy below it was. "It reeked," the editor told me at the time, "of anti-Tory prejudice" – and for the remainder of that election I was in the dog-house.

I felt the disgrace all the more keenly as throughout the campaign I had been allowed a quite remarkable latitude. Although only twenty-five, I had been allotted the job of drawing up the notes of guidance – for the previous nine months I had been the paper's by-election reporter – for members of the editorial staff conducting what were known in those less psephological days as "constituency surveys". I took to the responsibility with all the brashness of youth and, though today (surveying that yellowing document) I shudder at the peremptory tone of the instructions I gave, Alastair – in that same volume in which I get chastised for my coverage of the Macmillan rally at Bellevue – was generous enough to remark that my constituency surveys memorandum became "an office classic".

That, though, was wholly typical of him. As an editor, he was not just an enabler but a great encourager. On a Friday evening he would quite often casually inquire whether one had any plans for the next day – and, if not, whether one would care to go out with him for "a hike" round the Peak District in Derbyshire. As an *al fresco* experience, it did not always turn out to be unmitigated pleasure: as the rain slashed down, he would stride determinedly forward past the welcome dry and warmth of roadside pubs, implacable in his resolution to reach the number of miles he had set himself to meet as a target in a given space of time. Nevertheless, on those sometimes rugged outings he always treated you as a total equal – talking freely not just about political and public affairs but also about the more delicate problems he faced in the office, discussing the latter with a quite remarkable frankness and candour. Only years afterwards did it occur to me that, with the somewhat innocent boy scout side to his character, he probably felt closer to young reporters of my age than he did to those in the official hierarchy of the paper (who, for the most part, were people a great deal older than he was). There was certainly never any "side" to him – and, though in the reporters' room we used occasionally to mock his essentially temperate approach to life (his idea of a drink, we used to say, was a glass of lemonade), it was almost always done with amused affection.

Later on, of course, with all the initial difficulties of the London printing and the very real threat in 1966 of the paper's forced merger with the *Times*, problems were to crowd in upon him, and he necessarily became a more remote figure to younger members of the *Guardian* staff than he had been in those early Manchester days. But I shall always be glad that I first knew him then in his youthful prime – and never be shy of boasting that anything I know about journalism I learnt at his feet.

Alastair at home in Bridge of Allan, near Stirling

The family: before Alastair was born
Back row from left: Howard, Winnie, Hector (Alastair's father), Alison (Alastair's mother), Arnold
Front row from left: Dine, Scott (Alastair's brother), Jessie (Alastair's grandmother) with Alan in front, May (Arnold's wife) with Margot on knee, William Reid (Alastair's grandfather) with Micky leaning, and Aunt Jessie

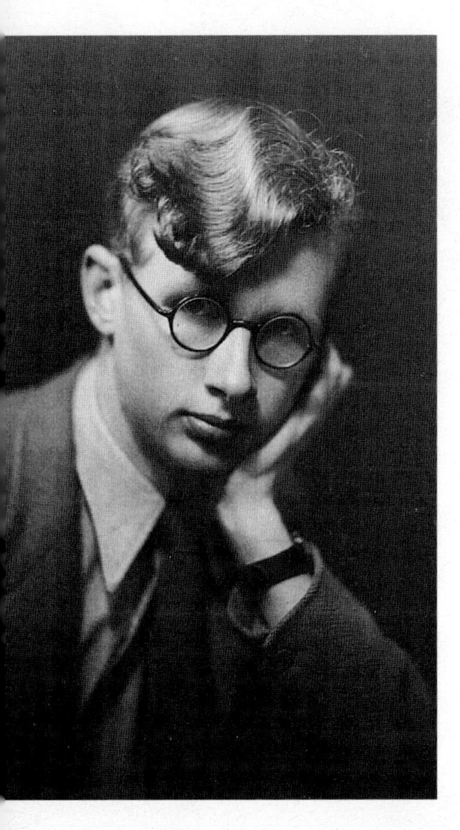

Left and below: Alastair as a schoolboy

Bottom: Alastair holding Lucy, Miranda with Tom in front, Alex beside Tom, Mary attempting to escape

Right: Alastair at work on Die Welt

Below: In the Guardian newsroom

Above: Editorial conference with Paddy Monkhouse second left

Right: Leaving the Guardian. The figure in the background is Peter Preston

Above: Alastair enjoying the outdoors
Below: Climbing his beloved Goat Fell (photograph by Denis Thorpe)
Opposite: On top of the Wade Stone on the A9 (photograph by Denis Thorpe)
Bottom right: At Dunadd making the documentary on Columba

Alastair and Sheila

The tank survived

Jean Stead

Two London editors were talking in Fleet Street in the early 1950s. I happened to hear them. One (from the *Glasgow Herald*) said: "You want to watch this young chap we've just lost to the *Guardian*. He's quite extraordinary. He's going to go far."

He did, quite soon. By 1956, Alastair was editor of the *Guardian* at the age of thirty-six, finding his way through the crises of Suez and the Hungarian revolution. In the Clachan, the pub next door to the Fleet Street office, the young reporters spoke gloomily of his abstemiousness and thrift – an orange–juice drinking Scot who felt in a purse for his small change, and if he was in a really wild mood, offered you a sherry. He asked all his staff to fill in cards setting out their special interests so he would best know how to deploy them. Two of them wrote that their main interests were public houses, though that was the last time they ever tried to take a rise out of the formidable new editor.

For Alastair was not only awash with the spirit of C.P. Scott, the paper's greatest editor, but set out clearly and definitely to model himself on him. Take the qualities of C.P. as described by another great editor, W.P. Crozier, in the authorised biography by J.L. Hammond: "The moral principles applied with great fidelity, liberty combined with high moral earnestness required in *Guardian* journalists, distrust of alcohol and gambling, a passion for clear English with correct grammar and the writing of reproachful notes to culprits when they did not come up to grammatical scratch, a great love of the outdoors, thrift, and courtesy to all staff combined with great authority". Anyone who worked for Alastair Hetherington on the *Guardian* will recognise those qualities in him too. For most of the time he succeeded in following his role model.

The authority came effortlessly – after all, he had been a wartime tank commander. This made working for him as a department head seem secure and simple. He was secure enough himself to listen carefully to the other point of view. He made an almost obsessive virtue of tolerance. Outright authority he used rarely and when he did, though it might be frustrating, it was also reassuring. You knew the tank stood a good chance of surviving.

At one point, though, it didn't. What few of us knew in the sixties and early seventies was that Alastair was hampered by the private fight he was waging to stop the attempts of C.P.'s grandson, Laurence Scott, the company chairman, to close the *Guardian* or merge it with the *Times*. He knew the merger would mean the loss of the journalists' freedom, the radical leader line and the social concerns, to the ingrained conservatism of the *Times*.

Even as he was following the reforming traditions of the *Guardian*'s founder, John Edward Taylor, who had started the paper with ten friends putting up £100 each in 1821 (after the slaughter of the weavers at the Battle of Peterloo), Hetherington knew that its very survival was being threatened. He even allowed himself to be drawn into talks on a merger, but he was soon leading the campaign to save the *Guardian* from merger and closure with the support of Richard Scott, chairman of the Scott Trust. The closure threat continued into the seventies, as the circulation mounted, along with company debts. Few of the journalists knew.

The circulation doubled under his editorship, reaching towards the 400,000 daily sales it manages today. But the rising circulation brought rising costs. The paper had no money, but there was a deep commitment to radical traditions. There was a new hard edge to the investigative reporting Alastair was called on to handle when the intake of reporters was at its peak in the 1970s. Some, including the political correspondent, Ian Aitken, were recruited from the Beaverbrook newspapers, others from the sharpest talents of the Northcliffe newspapers, traditionally famous for news sense.

Once at the *Guardian*, their commitment to a paper that respected their integrity and judgement was even greater than that of the traditional intake from the provincial press and Oxbridge. They knew how lucky they were, and worked well alongside established *Guardian* journalists like Harold Jackson, Simon Winchester, Simon Hoggart and Adam Raphael. There were also Australians, who brought their usual pioneering attitude to the newsroom – time to shake up the *Guardian* and the old country, was their attitude, and they were right.

C.P. Scott never had to deal with anything like this. But Alastair enjoyed it, developing a taste for the competitiveness of news. The paper's Fleet Street reputation rose with its sales. Night and day we sweated over how best to beat the opposition – and we regarded the whole of Fleet Street as the opposition.

Alastair and his new night editor, Brian Jones, would together watch *News at Ten*, determined that readers should not be served up with a diet of news already over-digested from the evening newspapers and television. There had to be a sense of surprise in the front page, important stories must be thrown forward from the previous night's headlines, and exclusives used whenever possible. The demand and encouragement for journalists to produce exclusives was unremitting.

Judgement of news was based on informed insight into the effects of the policy issues of the day. Alastair liked to talk to his staff about government in the widest sense at his orange juice staff get-togethers in the editor's room. By this he meant demonstrating how government policy could affect every issue of a person's life. A housing law passed with little publicity could result in families being evicted from high-rent slums by Peter Rachman's men and their alsatians in order to force even higher rents. A heartless government policy in the Caribbean combined with a search for low-cost labour in England resulted in the scenes shown on the BBC2 documentary *Windrush* – West

Indians arriving without proper clothing or any housing, to be exploited and then persecuted by police and public.

The news and features desks followed that approach. It led to a daily digging over obscure lines of agency copy or buried paragraphs in rival newspapers, which often would reveal enough to start an investigation.

In one story, known as "the leaks case" the source was a routine press conference. The then Liberal MP, John Pardoe, said that private inquiry agents were claiming they could obtain criminal records from the Criminal Records Office, people's bank statements from the banks, and tax returns from the Inland Revenue, as well as other personal information.

Only the *Guardian* followed this up, thanks to the diligence of a determined former *Newsweek* reporter who had covered the Vietnam war, Peter Harvey. He set out to get the evidence.

He found it, but it was days before Alastair allowed it to go into the paper. For the sake of the *Guardian's* reputation, he insisted it had to be rock solid. It was published only after Peter Harvey had finally passed the test of finding out from the inquiry agent Alastair's personal tax returns, which he did himself.

Next morning there was a call for Peter Harvey from the head of the civil service, Sir William Armstrong, and a summons to meet him. Soon, the heavy boots of a criminal investigation squad were stomping down the newsroom corridor to Alastair's room, their owners ready to grill us and take our fingerprints. And Alastair was in for a tense tea party in the garden of No. 10 Downing Street with the prime minister, Ted Heath.

Imagine the polite chink of china as Alastair confided to Ted that he wasn't used to the rough and impolite handling of these former robbery squad detectives. They were trying to get Peter's source, and in the process having our telephones tapped, Alastair followed, and no doubt his mail opened. No sympathy stirred Sir Edward's immobile features. "You have broken the Official Secrets Act, Alastair," he said. "If you don't co-operate with the police you will just have to go to prison."

Alastair didn't go to prison. Peter Harvey won the British Press Awards reporter of the year award for the story and later Alastair won the journalist of the year award. An official inquiry into the leaks was launched. The private inquiry agent went to prison and said later that he had found it hard to sit in his cell and read about the award – but we had not knowingly betrayed him.

Alastair was the outstanding editor of his era, overlooked by history until now. He was in the classic tradition, with one foot in public life and the other in whatever happened to interest him and his staff at the time. He left a huge space for worlds they found interesting – rock music, archaeology, the new youth culture. He was unfettered by the new modern management culture, so often self-censoring in its choice of subjects and writers.

He took on Martin Walker, later the award-winning Moscow and then Washington correspondent, as an untried journalist in an office full of experienced men and women. It was not only because of his brilliant academic record (always a strong selling point with Alastair), but because he had been at the Woodstock festival in the United States, acted as senatorial aide for Ed Muskie in the presidential campaign, and, with his beads and kaftans, unashamedly flaunted the spirit of the 1960s generation emerging into the 1970s.

He was probably the first editor to take the youth culture seriously. His strong liberal instincts and serious purpose were always open to new ideas. He shocked senior staff by backing American action in Vietnam and internment in Northern Ireland, but listened to their arguments and retained their respect. His editorship saw the first major design changes for the *Guardian*.

He has always been a complicated man, passionate but very private about his ideas, self-controlled to a degree. There was a seam of tragedy in his editorship. Fifteen years after his departure, strained and exhausted by the continual financial crises, to be controller of BBC Scotland, the *Guardian's* fortunes changed. A windfall of £70m from a flotation of Reuters shares enabled the paper at last to pay off all its debts and mortgages. The marketing and management had been modernised, *Guardian* editors, like C.P. Scott, were once again free to take part in business decisions and those affecting the security of the paper through membership of the Scott Trust. Publication of stories which might bring expensive legal costs, like the Jonathan Aitken libel case, need no longer threaten the paper's very survival.

When he went in 1975, a wave of shock and loss ran through the building. Alastair himself wrote, in his book *Guardian Years*: "I missed the *Guardian* greatly, as I knew I would. I missed the companionship of men and women of sharp intellect, political acumen, cheerful irreverence and yet serious purpose. I missed the stimulus of news, of never knowing what topic would dominate the next day's work and of getting the paper out every night." He missed us and we missed him. We feared that the radical C.P. Scott era had faded forever.

On into the blizzard

Peter Gibbings

I first met Alastair Hetherington in the Arts Council's offices in a corner of St James's Square. It was 1966 and the occasion was the last attempt to hold together a consortium of the *Guardian* and *Manchester Evening News*, the *Observer* and Claud Morris, a man who was driven by a strong dislike of Roy Thomson because of what he felt had been an unfair business deal. Its objective was to counter bid for the *Times* against Roy Thomson, who it was felt if successful would threaten both the *Guardian* and the *Observer*. It was, however, fatally flawed because the basis of the plan was that if the bid succeeded the *Times* and the *Guardian* would be merged. Laurence Scott, chairman of the *Guardian* and *Manchester Evening News*, supported the idea but Alastair most certainly did not. He it was who rallied the *Guardian* editorial and the Scott Trust under the chairmanship of Richard Scott to oppose the proposal. This had resulted a few days previously in Laurence having to telephone David Astor, the *Observer's* editor and confess that he had been "turned over".

The meeting at the Arts Council under Lord Goodman's chairmanship did not last long, but it lasted long enough for me to become aware of Alastair's strength of character and determination that whatever adversity it faced, the *Guardian* should remain independent.

Roy Thomson, of course, succeeded in buying the *Times* and I thought that was the end of the matter, until early in 1967 Alastair telephoned me at the *Observer* where I was the deputy manager and asked if I would come to lunch. We met at the Athenaeum and over a simple meal he asked me if I would become managing director of the *Guardian* and a director of the parent company. At the time it seemed a foolish thing to even contemplate – leaving the comparative safety of the *Observer* for the very obvious hazards of trying to help turn round the weak and ailing *Guardian*. However, Alastair's strong belief in the paper and his own forcé of character and obvious integrity led me forty-eight hours later to say yes. It shortly transpired that his approach to me was largely his own initiative and others in the company, particular Kenneth Searle, the then managing director of the group, had somewhat different ideas. However, Alastair got his own way and in the middle of 1967 I joined the *Guardian*. This started a long, successful and, from my point of view, very rewarding partnership between us, during which the *Guardian* was rescued from its dire condition and set on the path towards the strong position it holds today.

Following the decision in 1966 to keep the *Guardian* independent, it had become necessary to cut back its costs heavily. The brunt of this cost-cutting had unfairly fallen on the editorial department and Alastair and I agreed on the extreme urgency of rebuilding it, so that the paper could at least start to compete with the rampant *Times* which, gorging on Thomson money, was rapidly expanding and heading for a circulation in excess of 500,000 copies while we struggled at around 270,000 copies.

In the early days we certainly had some disagreements. Alastair, on one occasion, quoted at me C.P. Scott's dictum that the editor and manager should walk hand in hand together but with the editor always one pace ahead. I rejected that and said we had to be equal, respecting each other's abilities in our separate areas, but working together to achieve a common objective. This was totally contrary to Alastair's natural instincts and the *Guardian*'s traditions, but he accepted it nevertheless as the basis of our partnership. As the symbol of this, he agreed that we should share the chairmanship of Guardian

Newspapers, the operating company, each of us taking the chair at alternate meetings. I shudder to think what C.P. Scott would have said about that!

Early on, I learnt that one of his greatest strengths was his intellectual integrity. He might not and often did not like some of my proposals, but if the logic of the argument led to a particular conclusion, he would swallow his dislike, colouring up a little as he did so and agree to it. For my part, I tried to do the same and so our trust in each other grew.

From the point of view of keeping to his budget, he was a manager's joy. Cut to the bone as his resources were, he never overspent without, at the very least, consulting me and if I felt I had reluctantly to say no because of lack of funds, then he would accept it. Sometimes we did a little bartering. His strong desire was to rebuild the foreign coverage of the paper which had suffered badly in the cutbacks. Mine was to make the paper more comprehensive so as to appeal to a wider audience. This meant in particular strengthening our city and sports coverage which, for instance, carried no horse racing at all, although that was an omission which certainly did not worry Alastair. He was always asking me for the money to have a correspondent at the United Nations and so the day came when, following his reiteration of that request, I said he could have his man at the United Nations if I could have a man on Epsom Downs. Much to my amazement he agreed and so horse racing came back to the *Guardian* after an absence of over seventy years. On its re-introduction it formed the basis of a very successful sales drive.

He was completely fearless in his campaign on matters which he felt vitally important, but nevertheless always warned me about what he proposed to do and would listen carefully to my assessment of its possible impact on our revenues. In practice, I always supported him because we both believed that there was no point in publishing the *Guardian* at a loss if it was not true to itself in major matters.

When it came to hard work, Alastair never spared himself and had amazing stamina. Long hours in the London office were followed by the night train to Manchester so that he could keep in personal touch with the journalists still working in what had been, until the mid-'60s, the *Guardian's* head office. Then he would once again board the night train and be back in London by the following morning.

He was a man who placed great store on getting the details of something right. Accuracy mattered greatly to him and this attitude, it seemed to me, was reflected in his small, neat handwriting which he employed to take detailed notes of all his discussions. He had a tape recorder mind and after a conversation with, say, a leading politician, he would return to the office and at once dictate a comprehensive *aide-mémoire,* which was then meticulously filed away to be drawn on at any time in the future for a leader or opinion piece. What a mine of information those notes would be for a political historian.

He never dabbled in the flesh pots so beloved by the denizens of Fleet Street. If you were going out to lunch with him you walked at an extremely brisk pace from Gray's Inn Road to the Athenaeum – a distance of nearly two miles – and then back again along the Embankment. I remember on one occasion when we were returning from a lunch in mid-winter. There was a bitter wind blowing and it started to snow heavily. Suddenly a large Rolls Royce pulled up at the kerb and from its luxurious depth we heard the voice of Peter Jenkins, our star columnist, who had obviously been offered a lift back in comfort by the important personage he had been lunching with. "Get in," he said, "and I'll take you back to the office." "No, thank you," replied Alastair without hesitation and strode rapidly on into the blizzard, leaving me panting somewhat unhappily in his wake.

Such austerity and devotion to duty inevitably made some people regard him as cold and unfeeling. However, this was far from the truth. He was, underneath his tough Scottish exterior, a warmhearted family man always most considerate and courteous to everyone. But he would allow nothing to divert him from his drive to ensure the survival of the *Guardian.*

He succeeded and the *Guardian* slowly prospered – at least in comparative terms – as our personal relationship grew. By the time we celebrated our 150th anniversary in May 1971 with a spectacular dinner at the Dorchester – *that* certainly stretched the budget a little – we were selling over 300,000 copies and were slightly ahead of the *Times*. By any standard it was a great achievement and on a night when Willy Brandt and Ted Heath, then prime minister, were our chief speakers, topped up by the inimitable Arnold Goodman, Alastair went out of his way in his own speech to praise most generously the contribution management had made to the miracle.

When he finally left in 1975 to become controller of BBC Scotland, his achievements over nineteen very difficult years as editor of the *Guardian* were there for all to see. In a speech I made at his farewell dinner, I said, among other things, that if I was in a really tight corner in a battle, there was no-one with whom I would rather stand side by side than Alastair. He would never flinch and never let you down until the victory was won.

Backstabbing and intrigue, big money and low morals have always constituted the classic Fleet Street scenario. Alastair Hetherington shone out as a wonderful example – and there must be very few – of a successful editor who never subscribed to any of that. By his leadership, hard work, integrity and fearlessness he played the leading part in first saving and then establishing on firm foundations the *Guardian* as a national newspaper. All who work on the paper, the Scott Trust who own it, and its countless loyal readers across the world owe him a deep debt of gratitude.

The patterns he taught

Peter Preston

When I write about Alastair, I write inevitably about myself too: and about how I came to understand. In the beginning – as a junior reporter in Cross Street or a fledgling specialist correspondent in the dark and steamy hulk of Gray's Inn Road – you only glimpsed the editor of the *Guardian* from time to time. He would walk through the newsroom, but he would rarely stop. His office door was closed, guarded by ladies of a certain ferocity. You knew he was there because, as night fell, you could look up from the street and see his office lights still shining.

But then, a decade on, it was I who was the editor of the *Guardian*, the burner of the midnight oil: and what he had done, what in many senses he'd endured, became far clearer to me. I was sitting in his chair. I was living his life. The thoughts and the problems which came piling in were old friends he had learned to live with. So there are two Alastairs in the memory: the one I saw from the back stalls and the one I came to know, and appreciate still more, when he was gone, home to Scotland.

Back stalls boy arrived with reference attached. I'd been working, after university, in Liverpool on the *Daily Post*: three years in the Jeans family salt mines. Where did you go from there? A natural transition. Chris Driver – a trainee the year before – had slid over to Manchester. Peter Eckersley, the talent

I most admired, was heading that way. I'd always read the *Guardian*. I wrote out of the blue and got an interview with Harry Whewell, the news editor. It went well. He fixed a slot with Mr Hetherington.

The dramatic thing to say – the walk down the heavy panelling of the corridor, the knock on the frosted door, the meeting with the ruddy-faced man in the shirtsleeves – was that it was the encounter that changed my life. But in fact (as again I came to understand later) it was short and slightly taciturn. He was busy. He was doing what editors do, making sure that the man someone down the line wanted to hire didn't raise prickles of alarm. At any rate, I came stamped with approval.

And then began a magical mystery tour of jobs. Was Manchester the main office, or London? Perhaps the true heart of the paper was where Alastair seemed to be most of the time: on the night sleeper to Euston. But in transition there was also opportunity. I'd done political stuff in Liverpool. The by-elections started to come my way. The editor was cornered on some radio show. Had the glory gone from Cross Street? Not at all, he said: why, it would continue to be the talent pool for foreign reporting. Good news. The president of Ghana had challenged the *Guardian* to monitor his latest referendum. Arthur Hopcraft and I were whisked away to West Africa. Then Michael Wall in Cyprus needed a break. I got there, too. One Sunday morning when I was at home with my parents in Leicestershire, Alastair called. Could I move to London in three weeks flat? We needed a new education correspondent. Came the 1966 crisis and the orders changed again. Gerry Fay had gone from the diary column. Replacement needed instantly: replacement found. And thereafter I was features editor.

Looking back, there were five jobs of infinite variety over a span of seven years. At the time I accepted them gratefully, as though doled out by some fickle hand of fate. But towards the end I began to know better than that. Alastair had seen something in me he clearly thought worth developing. When I looked around, he was good at that. Geoffrey Moorhouse and Terry Coleman and Derek Malcolm and David McKie weren't the accidental heart of Features. They'd arrived and prospered in an environment which gave them room to breathe. And

News, twenty yards away, was just the same. He didn't have much money. He had to scrape every resource in those days of constant change and crisis. He was not a patroller. You wouldn't look up from your desk and suddenly find him there. But he was a great creator of context, the builder of an environment where talent could grow.

It would be wrong to say I knew him, at least for most of the time. There was always the professional reserve editors need to possess naturally or to cultivate – you can't have friends because you can't have favourites. In Features though, and later when I was production editor, putting the paper to bed at night, you had the chance to see him more closely in action. Though, in his clipped Scottish way, he seemed cool, he could turn suddenly fiery. Not lastingly so, and usually over policy things rather than practical things: but his neck would begin to redden and his mouth tighten. He cared about policies – about bombs and Vietnam or Ulster – in a way that absorbed attention. He might be right in the end (he often was) or wrong (that, too) but he cared and he was always thorough and thoughtful. There was no dumbing down. The leader writers' room, six feet from my desk, seemed an interestingly different place to be. Sometimes it was convulsed, as when Frank Edmead left over Vietnam; sometimes it coasted languidly while Alastair, down the corridor, took the verdict of the day to himself; sometimes – Northern Ireland times – the tensions spread wider, consuming debate in huddled corners. But it was great. It meant that what the paper said was important. It meant we were serious, there for something.

As heads of department, we'd gather at intervals to cement that seriousness – usually in one of those great old railway hotels Alastair had a curious passion for (soup, meat and two veg, a gooey sweet) where the agenda for the month was mapped out. The sessions were inclusive in a formal way. There were topics. You spoke to them. He took (and circulated) notes. You were involved, in that he wrote down and remembered what you said. Sometimes the business was purely practical. What did we use for our autumn push? How did we cope with the price going up – again? Sometimes, and just as compulsively, we'd launch into debate about the entrails of

Wilsonian government or Heath's post-Selsdon men. At the time, maybe, it all seemed a trifle academic (a mirror of the university life he'd learned from his father). At the time, the shrewd balancing act wasn't apparent. But such things fell into context later, for they were intrinsically about creating a proper context. They let you sense his mood and purpose, but they also allowed you the maximum freedom to be creative yourself.

I rarely met him one on one. Meetings were meetings. The important conversations happened on the hoof. "Let's go for a walk," he'd say, and he would pound off up Gray's Inn Road. We might have a sandwich in a little cafe just across from Euston or sit on a bench in a graveyard. Those were the times that moves took place. Could I handle Features? (After Chris Driver.) Would I, later, like to be an all-purpose assistant editor? (I wouldn't: I'd rather learn about the hardest end of hard news night after night.) He seldom seemed rattled. Once, I thought, when the new management wanted the paper re-designed by our ad agency and he clearly felt under pressure. "Do you see what they want to do?" he said, unrolling the dummies. And once, towards the end, we had a lousy little row over sub-heads on front page briefs. I thought I knew about lay-out. So did he. But all the time, without realising it, I was learning from him. I was his student.

Somewhere around his seventeenth year of editing you could sense a restless distancing. The door was closed tighter. The absences were more frequent. He was looking, psychologically, for the next challenge. Yet when, suddenly, he was off at last – to BBC Scotland – there was still the sudden shock of separation, and opportunity. I was thirty-five. It had not, in any true sense, occurred to me that I might be editor. He helped me to realise that I had a chance, and that is one more thing that I owe him.

But the real appreciation came, as I say, only in the months and years after he had departed. There was the loneliness, the feeling of weight on your shoulders. There was the tyranny of the 'phone, ringing day and night. There was the hidden world of management – of boards struggling to make ends meet and trusts trying to do the right thing. There was the endless, menacing blight of unions cutting up rough.

The words on newsprint were, and are, the easy bits of

editing. It is the words behind the boardroom door that are difficult – and the tasks that editors get no credit for, like hiring brilliant people who, naturally, take that credit to themselves. Alastair fought some epic boardroom battles. He brought the paper to London and gave it the chance to become the *Guardian*. He saved it from extinction, with courage and tenacity, when that gamble was almost failing. His two decades were full of triumphs large and small.

How can anyone who was there at the time forget? I can't do that. Some of the things I did next were reaction to him, deliberate by design. He'd been the friend and confidante of politicians. I did not want that. He had kept the most astonishing, meticulous records. I couldn't do that. He had stayed clear of the nightly fray. I rolled my sleeves up on the desk.

But, even in reaction, I knew I was acknowledging his example, and his continuing presence. Editors come and go rarely on the *Guardian*: just five this century. As they depart, the paper remains and goes on, so that they seem to live only in the memory of those who worked with them. Inevitable – yet not quite as simple as that. Good newspapers are like good families. They develop rituals and rhythms of their own. They appoint journalists who stay over decades. There are things they do that they would have never have thought of if some editor, long ago, had not laid the first foundation. On all these counts, today's *Guardian* is also Alastair's *Guardian*. He was an editor to remember with pride: and I remember him every time I pick the paper from the mat, turn the pages and see the patterns he left and the patterns he taught.

Sir

Adam Raphael

My first meeting with Alastair Hetherington was almost my last. As a young lad on the make whose journalistic career had so far been limited to covering parish councils for the *Swindon Evening Advertiser*, I had applied to the *Guardian* for a job. John Cole, the then news editor, whose blunt Ulster accent hid a warm heart, suggested after a brief chat that I should be wheeled in to see the boss.

Alastair did his best to put me at ease, asking what my particular interests were. I immediately made a big mistake saying that I was keen on defence. "Ah," said Alastair, "have you read Macnamara's Congressional testimony on the strategic defence initiative?" I had just about heard of Robert Macnamara but I hadn't got a clue about his evidence to the defence committee. After a few more probing questions, none of which I could answer, I was sent out. Alastair, understandably, was not impressed, remarking mildly that I didn't seem to know much. According to John Cole, the following exchange then took place: "Come off it, Alastair, no one has read Macnamara's testimony apart from you." "Oh well, perhaps he will do." On that equivocal basis, I was hired.

The *Guardian* in those days was run a bit like a regiment with the editor as a kindly but distant colonel. At least, that was how it seemed to this junior reporter with recent memories of national service. I took to calling Alastair, "sir", a practice that could have been construed as either insolence or respect. It certainly annoyed Alastair. One day, he turned to me and said in clipped Scottish tones: "For goodness sake, drop the sir." But for many months, I couldn't. Alastair was a natural commander-in-chief and we subalterns were naturally a bit in awe. In those days, of course, I didn't have all that much contact but one saw enough to appreciate his virtues as an editor.

The paper did not make much money but it ran remarkably smoothly. Alastair had a series of trusted departmental chiefs, Geoffrey Taylor, John Cole, Christopher Driver and Harford Thomas and they were allowed to get on with their fiefdoms with little interference. The result was a remarkably unbitchy atmosphere. Power struggles, endemic in most papers, were confined to the fringe. Alastair was a good editor because he realised that once you got the right structure and the right people, the paper largely ran itself. Though shy and reserved, his integrity commanded respect from all those who worked with him. He prized good writing. Woe betide a sub-editor who, without consultation, altered a journalist's copy. The writer was king and it showed. In this collegiate atmosphere, talented writers flourished: Geoffrey Moorhouse, Harry Jackson, Terry Coleman, Philip Hope-Wallace, Neville Cardus and many others. Perhaps the competitive pressures were less in those days, though they didn't seem so, but there was space for unconventional thoughts.

There was also room for eccentrics, which attracted me. The *Guardian* has always had a tradition of appointing distinctly odd motoring correspondents. The chief qualification for the job was, if not a positive dislike of cars, a keen ambivalence about their social merits. When a vacancy arose, I was thus well suited. My immediate predecessor, J.R.L. Anderson, a noted scholar, had gone off in an alarmingly unseaworthy boat to retrace a Viking voyage. After that he had no wish to continue testing the latest models from Dagenham.

The late 1960s were a time of big profits, lavish expense accounts and much optimism in the car industry. With profits so fat, a big chunk of the marketing effort was directed at the dozen or so motoring correspondents who wrote for the national newspapers. We were wined, dined, flattered and generally spoilt. Understandably we were not popular. "The *reductio ad absurdum* of all journalism" was Bernard Levin's description of our trade. In those days of lavish advertising budgets, the manufacturers would launch their latest model by chartering a plane to fly the assembled motoring hacks to some exotic location like Outer Patagonia where we were entertained with belly dancers and lots of alcohol.

The manufacturers on the whole took a cynical view of that well-known doggerel: "You cannot hope to bribe or twist the honest British journalist. For seeing what the man unbribed will do, there's simply no occasion to." To lubricate publicity wheels that might need just a spot of oil, they showered gifts on us, mostly small items such as attache cases, rugs and ties but sometimes reaching the heights of rally jackets, tape recorders and tyres. After eighteen months of this high-living decadence, I was asked by *Punch* to write an article telling all. So under the title "Confessions of a motoring correspondent", I listed all the bribes I had been offered and – regrettably – had accepted. My dubious rationale was that no car manufacturer in his right mind would think it worth trying to bribe the motoring correspondent of the *Guardian.*

Shortly after the article appeared in *Punch*'s autumn issue celebrating the annual Earl's Court motor show, I was summoned by Alastair. He had *Punch* open in front of him, and he clearly didn't find my article as funny as I meant it to be for he asked with a trace of steel in his voice: "Don't you know that the paper has a house rule about gifts?" "No," I replied nervously. "What is it?" The answer was succinct: a *Guardian* reporter could accept only gifts that could be consumed within twenty four hours. As tyres, tape recorders and the like clearly fell outside this sensible guideline, the next question was perhaps inevitable: "I think you have been doing this motoring job long enough, don't you?" The upshot was that I was transferred from writing about cars and sent to the United States as one of the paper's foreign correspondents. For a motoring hack in disgrace, it was a fair sentence.

In Washington where I was stationed for the next few years, I did not have much contact with Alastair, apart from occasional encouraging notes he sent. In the midst of the Anguilla affair, a high-drama Caribbean farce, involving the British navy landing marines on a tiny peaceful island, I remember receiving a letter of commiseration from him. I had made friends with one of the island's local beauties, a lady called Ethelreda, and had written a glowing feature about her. When the paper finally reached the island some weeks later, the Gruaniad had changed her name to Ethelred. Even more occasionally, Alastair would arrive in Washington on a flying visit. I remember one such visit when he kindly said he would like to take me out to lunch. My eyes lit up at the thought of a lavish spread at one of the city's fashionable and expensive restaurants. No such luck. At the appointed hour, I was steered firmly by Alastair towards a snack bar.

That was the trouble with having such a plain-living editor; he set such a parsimonious example that the expenses of all *Guardian* reporters (with the notable exception of Peter Jenkins) were notoriously low. Walking with Alastair around Washington in the heat of summer was also an exhausting affair. Tremendously fit from having climbed the Munros, he would set off at a great pace, talking almost as fast. Not only was it difficult to keep up, it was also difficult to follow what he was saying because he often assumed that one knew much more than one did.

After five years in Washington, Alastair rightly suggested that it was time that I came home before I became totally Americanised. But as I had a lot of holiday owing and still had a passion to see more of the world, I asked whether I could spend some time in South Africa, taking Caroline, my South African wife, and our one-year-old son, Thomas, with me. Alastair agreed and was very supportive when I suggested that it might be worth taking a look at how British companies in South Africa were treating their African workforces.

What I didn't realise, until I arrived in Capetown, was the size and difficulty of this task. It was rumoured that many British companies operating in South Africa were paying wages that were below the minimum level needed for a family to survive in reasonably good health. But how to prove it? I compiled a questionnaire which I sent to the largest British companies asking them detailed questions about their employment practices. Details of those companies who declined to respond had to be acquired painfully and slowly by standing outside factory gates and asking workers for their pay slips. Without the help of black South African trade unions, academic researchers and locally based journalists, I wouldn't have got far. But after two months' hard work, I had enough information to confront some of the companies. The answers were revealing. The personnel director of Illovo Sugar Estates, which was paying its contract workers 55p a day, told me: "This is not magnificent but you have to remember these Bantu are mostly illiterate. And they are unproductive at first – we have to build them up. At home they just lie around and have a good time."

I arrived back in Britain at the beginning of March 1973, convinced that I had an important story to tell. On March 12, the *Guardian* ran the story on its front page across three columns, "British Firms Pay Africans Starvation Rate", naming dozens of blue-chip companies as having paid below-subsistence wages.

Alastair from the start had been a firm supporter of mine but neither he nor I, nor indeed anyone else on the paper, realised the seriousness of the risks we were running. When I came into the office the next day, they quickly became apparent as several of the named companies issued denials. When the writs began to arrive, Alastair's confidence understandably began to be shaken. With my sources thousands of miles away and the only evidence to support my story several scruffy notebooks filled with my indecipherable handwriting, I felt under considerable pressure. Two companies, in particular, were leading the protest pack. Alastair was sufficiently impressed by their emphatic denials that he insisted that the paper should publish retractions despite my vehement opposition.

When I found out that one of the companies had increased its pay rates by 30% on the day of the publication of my article, I was furious and let fly in a bitter private memo to Alastair. Harsh words were exchanged between us. It was almost the only time we fell out. "You are the most arrogant man I have ever dealt with," Alastair said in exasperation, after I had accused him of bending too easily to pressure. Depressed and overwrought, I considered resigning but I was talked out of it.

It was the lowest point. From that moment, things began to

look up. A leading article in the *Times* actually praised the *Guardian's* campaign, a view echoed by several papers in South Africa. Sensing the tide of public opinion, many of the leading companies announced an immediate inquiry into their South African employment practices, and promised that in future they would pay all their workers above subsistence levels. These public statements were followed by a spate of extraordinary wage increases.

These dramatic wage increases were undoubtedly spurred on by the decision of the Commons select committee on trade and industry, led by Bill Rodgers, to mount an inquiry. The committee's report, published a year later after hearing evidence from thirty major British companies with interests in South Africa and written evidence from a further 100 companies, concluded that many firms had been grossly underpaying their South African workers, and recommended that a code of conduct should be established.

Looking back on this episode, I can see I was very unfair to Alastair. Few editors would have been so supportive, or prepared to place as much trust as he did in a relatively junior reporter whose evidence to back up his claims was, to put it kindly, decidedly skimpy. Though he insisted that retractions should be published, the paper continued to back the general thrust of what I had written and to campaign against poverty wages. All this was not without cost. The growth in display advertising which had been increasing steadily over a number of years suddenly flattened out. The legal actions also absorbed a huge amount of executive time. It was typical of Alastair that I was never reproached for errors of fact and judgement which made things much more difficult than they need have been.

What made him in my view a great editor was that he was both brave and fair. He commanded loyalty because he was prepared to fight the battles of those who worked for him. I have no doubt that the success of today's *Guardian* owes much to his tolerant and open-minded leadership. I look back on his distinguished editorship with great affection as do all those who worked with me at that time. We were in good hands, and we knew it.

Lunch in trousers

Linda Christmas

It started badly. I wrote to Alastair Hetherington asking for a job as a reporter in 1970. He wrote back saying that there were no vacancies but that he had passed my letter on to Mary Stott, editor of the women's page: there might be a chance of freelance work. I groaned and threw the letter to one side. I'd just come back from an inspirational first visit to New York: the place was buzzing with women aching to be "liberated" from ghettos.

A few weeks later, the pragmatist took over. If that was going to be my route into the *Guardian*, so be it. Once inside I could at least try to change attitudes. I wrote for the women's page and six months later was offered a job by the features editor, Peter Preston. My brief was to write mainly for the women's page but also for other feature pages. I didn't meet AH.

On my first day at the *Guardian* in September 1971 there was an emergency chapel meeting. I trundled off with the rest, only to discover that the meeting was about me. My copy was to be blacked because AH had not advertised the job which had been given to me. It was to be blacked until AH agreed not to do it again! Funny old world. Fiery first day. I still didn't meet AH.

To me, at the age of twenty-seven, he seemed intimidating. His reputation made him so. His independence of thought, his ability to stand alone in his views rather than follow the pack, was admirable. We all knew about Suez. His knowledge and experience was so respected that often he was called upon by politicians to share thoughts. This sometimes caused other *Guardian* folk to sneer. A few might have felt a genuine, journalistic, desire for distance from Downing Street, but for others the sneers were a cover for jealousy. I was then married to a young Conservative MP, Norman Fowler, and understood better than most journalists the symbiotic relationship between Fleet Street and Westminster. It was something Alastair and I were to discuss in years to come, but not for the moment.

It was not his style to get to know his staff. He did not wander round and chat. He was the last of the great non-interventionist editors. He stayed in his office and, I assumed, concerned himself with foreign affairs, defence issues, politics and leaders (as befits someone whose background was in leader writing, defence issues and foreign affairs). The rest he delegated.

That is not to suggest that he couldn't be bothered with the rest. He fully appreciated – and stated so in his book *Guardian Years* – that the women's page made a powerful contribution to the paper. It was, he said "an influence towards a more liberal, tolerant and equal society".

He didn't send many memos – I got only one. Several readers had written to him praising a full page article I had written about the work of paramedics in the New York police force. One of the letters suggested that the *Guardian* had found a "female Alistair Cooke." AH scrawled across the top: "quite right" and sent it to me. The letter is treasured: it contained the perfect compliment.

It was eighteen months before we talked and, today, twenty five years later, I can recall vividly the moment he walked past my desk and said: "Come and have lunch with me and talk about the position of women." The features department went silent.

When the day came my colleagues commented on the fact that I was wearing trousers. "You are not going to lunch with the editor dressed in trousers are you?" I hadn't given it a thought, but others felt he would disapprove. They saw him as old-fashioned in his view of women. Nothing could be further from the truth. One of AH's many gifts was to see women as people.

Lunch was magic. We talked and talked. He was late back for the leader writers' conference. That did not go unnoticed. And what were we discussing? My name had been put forward to edit the women's page. I wanted to change the title to Guardian Miscellany (a title with deep roots in the *Guardian's* past). I argued that there were no such things as "women's issues"; merely issues that mainly interested women and other issues that mainly interested men. And in the years to come the gap between the two sets of interests would be eroded. The *Guardian* should encourage this and lead the way.

Men already read the page; more men would be encouraged to read it without the silly label and the removal of the label would also enable the page content to be less restricted. Radical stuff, or so it seemed then.

AH understood. He might have been some twenty five years older than I, a whole generation older, but he *listened* to new ideas. He understood the logic of my request but was worried about the reaction of both the advertising and circulation managers. In the end, he sanctioned my plan.

There were no more lunches. During the next few years he would occasionally stop by my desk for sixty seconds. Usually it was to pass on the comments of an outsider to whom he had been talking.

I'd written a curtain raiser on the Swedish elections: rumour had it that Olof Palme was going to lose office, but after a fascinating visit, I had written that he would retain office with the help of the Communist party. AH had met the Swedish ambassador who had said that I'd got it right. AH liked that.

He would also comment on pieces that I had commissioned. Those were the years when the frank discussion of sex and social relationships was an essential element of the page. Such articles were included because a newspaper ought to be, as Arthur Miller once said, "society talking to itself".

The changes, for good or ill, needed to be described and discussed. Jill Tweedie writing about wife-swapping parties caused a few comments. It seemed to me that AH, perceived as something of a puritan, was nonetheless happy to have his paper talked about so long as the talk was serious rather than sensational. We were serious. In those days, we were a touch frightened of being frivolous. Now alas it is the other way round.

It is a paradox that the man we saw as something of a puritan could be so at ease with the mood of the 1970s. I recall a conversation in Washington with Simon Winchester. Both our marriages were in difficulties and Simon, being miles from base, said to me, as I was about to return to London, "What will AH make of all this? Will he think the less of us?"

I tell the tale in order to show that we really cared what our editor thought of us and to show how little we understood him. Alastair was aloof, but a fine manager: he created a climate in which one could flourish, follow ideas, take risks. He gave me confidence. I hired James Cameron to write a column on a Monday, alternating with Jill Tweedie. I did this without consulting anyone. No one has such freedom now. I have often said that during my first three years at the *Guardian* I didn't have a job, I had a love affair.

When Alastair gave up the editorship, I was in Indonesia writing a travel article. I was glad to miss the turmoil over the succession. Little did I realise how much would change. Women's Guardian was restored and I was told to get rid of James Cameron. The readers, bless them, made sure that he survived.

We heard the news a few days before Christmas. I was sitting in the features department when the word went around that things had not worked out for Alastair at the BBC and that he was to leave Glasgow for Inverness. The comments were typical of journalists who delight in others' difficulties.

I said nothing. Instead I wrote a short note to Alastair saying how sorry I was to hear what had happened and that I hoped the people of Inverness realised how lucky they were. I then put the letter in my drawer. AH wouldn't remember who I was! I went home shocked by my lack of confidence in my own judgement. The next day I posted the letter. I immediately received a 'phone call from Alastair saying he was coming to London and would like to have lunch with me.

It was over this lunch, only the second that we had shared, that AH ceased to become my editor/former editor, and became my friend. It was a massive leap. Before long he was using our home in Islington as his London base. He soon became our favourite house guest, visiting frequently for two or three days at a time. He was organised and independent: if we were busy he looked after himself. My husband, John Higgins, was then arts editor of the *Times* so the diary was often crowded. It didn't matter. Nor did it matter that AH's interest in the arts was minimal.

He was the last of the big breakfasters and often cooked his own eggs and bacon – if he woke before this early riser. And he always forgot to clean the grill pan. Sometimes, he disrupted supper by his single-minded desire to watch the news or some programme that he needed to see (in the days before video recorders). And often, if there were other friends present, he would decide that he had had enough and take himself off to bed.

But grubby grill pans, and hefty doses of TV news, were a small price to pay for the pleasure of sharing his numerous interests and enthusiasms. He introduced me to the world of TV, to the need to question news values (while he was writing a book on the subject) and to the world of university journalism, both through his professorship at Stirling and his role as an external examiner at City University.

He was a profound influence on me. Can it be a coincidence that in time I was tempted to try television and work for *Newsnight*? Can it be a coincidence that I now teach at City University? He showed me the valuable role journalists could play in teaching the next generation.

He was a glorious teacher, so generous with his knowledge and his time: when I was accused of bias in a film I'd made for *Newsnight* about the 1987 Housing Bill, Alastair combed the twenty minute item, analysed every frame, measured every quote, and helped me prove that often bias is in the eye of the beholder.

When I told him that I was leaving the *Guardian* to write a book on Australia, he took a lively interest in the project and in a country that most people preferred to ignore. When I wrote my second book, on Thatcher's Britain, he introduced me to his beloved Scotland.

He lugged a dozen books to London for me to read. He helped plan my journey from the tip of Shetland to the Isle of Arran. We walked together in Orkney and talked of the Picts, we walked together in Stirling and dissected battles with the English; we walked in Arran and discussed nationalism. And when I had the idea of taking the oldest route from Scotland to Northern Ireland, by boat from Campbeltown, he didn't tell me I was daft, he tried to make it work for me. He tried everything to make it work for me, even persuading a friend to broadcast an appeal on Radio Clyde.

When he left the *Guardian* I'd been puzzled why he should want to return to Scotland, but not any more: he'd shared with me his love, understanding and commitment. And if I'd ever thought that sometimes his single minded commitment to his own work bordered on the selfish, this period in my life erased the thought. His desire to help with my book travelled further than Scotland. In the end he read the entire manuscript, painstakingly querying many details and helping me cut 30,000 words from the final draft.

I often ponder the complex question: what is friendship? When I do Alastair Hetherington slips easily to mind as a role model. We made no demands, but helped each other whenever we could. We were so at ease that we offered ourselves as "sounding boards". And we could disagree. He could discuss his committee meetings, his board meetings or whatever, knowing that not a syllable would be repeated.

We weren't always serious. My husband remembers our request for him to wear a kilt, when once we were staying in Arran. He did and looked dashing. But we were mostly serious. AH preferred a conversation of substance, with perhaps an hors d'oeuvre of gossip. Most journalists prefer to major in gossip and character assassination. A demeaning pastime. AH did not see every issue in black and white. His views were mostly leftish but sometimes a touch rightish. He could be both hawk and dove. I love this independent thinking: not for him the package deal of "left" or "right" beliefs clutched from cradle to grave. And I loved the fact that he was mercifully free of some *Guardian* prejudices: he didn't, for example, see all Tories as monsters.

When he met Sheila, he proved the point. When he decided to marry her he said to me: "I know you will understand – you married one too!" I admire his large family. I admired it even more when Sheila's children doubled its size: they all seem to get on so well.

Alastair Hetherington has been lucky. I didn't know Miranda, but I do know Sheila and marvel daily at her exceptional devotion. I have to say he deserves it.

I've been lucky too. I've enjoyed a bloody marvellous friendship.

Not very BBC

Ian Mackenzie

I was suspicious of the new controller. There he was in the *Daily Record* (even in black and white the red apple cheeks showed) poised to climb a mountain. How could someone so appallingly healthy have edited an intelligent newspaper all these years? Then I remembered. In 1968, working in London, I was producing a live religious current affairs programme for the ITV network and we invited Alastair to come and be quizzed on the ethics of his editorial on the Rhodesian crisis. His solution was straightforward: bomb Rhodesia. Aha, I thought, so he's coming to bomb BBC Scotland. Who will survive?

My Glasgow office looked onto Hamilton Drive. Day after day, my unease deepened as I witnessed my new boss striding out, possibly to a sandwich lunch in the Botanics, verbally and physically outpacing whichever younger colleague he was with. Dialoguing like mad, the younger colleague, in his twenties or thirties, would have curved spine, paunch, wrinkled skin, and careworn eyes. Alastair in his fifties had a complexion Demi Moore would die for, alcohol–free eyes, a broad grin, and a spring in his step most of us lose in our teens.

Worse was to come. It soon hit us that not only his physique indicated he'd come from another planet. Despite the evidence of mental activity in those disturbingly direct eyes, it became increasingly obvious that he had a limited grasp of BBC language. At its most basic, when he said "Please do this", he didn't understand that to mean, "Perhaps you might consider passing this from department to department, doing a memo, pushing it up your hierarchy, down again, and sideways to a committee." He actually meant "Do this." Such flying in the face of BBC tradition was ominous. A more serious flaw, from the BBC point of view, was that when Alastair said, "I will do this," he didn't mean he was delegating it to the great maw of the BBC machine. He actually intended to do it himself, probably that day. Who could live with such a person? Not the BBC. Not for long, anyway.

To say that his was a hands-on approach is to put it mildly. As one passed him – no, as he passed one – loping in shirt sleeves down a stairwell, there was no way of knowing whether he was on his way to have a fast philosophical exchange with a news editor or was rushing to the boiler–room to mend a fuse. If he had been captain of the Titanic, the iceberg would have been spotted sooner because Alastair (if he hadn't been stoking a boiler) would have been at the top of the mast with a telescope. But, if he was as new to the mechanics of liners as he was to the mechanics of broadcasting, he might have steered the ship enthusiastically into the iceberg; it would have been an exhilarating way to go.

Exhilarating it was. There was a certain sense that all this was rather hairy, but that was balanced by the fact that it was also rather fun. I exempt top management from that. For some of them it may have been a nightmare. But I wasn't in management. I was just head of the religious department. In those days, when the cult of management was but a cloud on the horizon, running a programme department was regarded as a creative activity. We were essentially producers, and Alastair's face to face approach was stimulating. He engaged producers in discussion as if programmes required cogitation. Suddenly there was a buzz at Queen Margaret Drive. It was the unusual sound made by brains having to work.

And watches had to work. Punctuality was discovered to be important. There was a certain style to a pre–Hetherington BBC meeting. People congregated at around the specified time. As coffee was poured, they gradually draped themselves round the room. Biscuits were passed round. The theme of the meeting was broached. One or two people would stroll in a little late and nod pleasantly to the chair and those in the group who were not outright enemies.

Alastair made it clear that this was not his way. He was there on the dot, and he began on the dot. He spoke with dispatch, he expected a debate, and he wanted a result. After the meeting, as often as not, he wrote his own *aide-mémoire*. It would be brief, crisp, and occasionally wrong. Wrong, because in the intensity of his desire to wake up a sleepy BBC machine and get things done, he didn't always appreciate that the actual processes of making a programme could be slow and messy,

On the *Guardian*, he'd worked to a twenty-four hour agenda, and now he had difficulty divesting himself of that sense of urgency – not least because his first year was preoccupied with news. The BBC had sent him to Glasgow to beef up the BBC's preparedness for devolution, if the projected referendum produced a positive result; and therefore a sharp and professional treatment of politics was a logical priority.

Although he was always courteous and affable to me, I had little intellectual connection with him in that first year. His interest in the religious department seemed largely confined to two things: the Churches; and *Thought for the Day*.

The Kirk particularly engaged him. That, too, made sense in political terms – the national church offered an established image of national identity. He whirled me to Edinburgh and back to renegotiate General Assembly arrangements with surprised grey suits at 121 George Street. "Whirled" is a moderate word for a process which involved the M8 passing in a blur. He was pushing himself and everyone else so hard, some middle managers thought the internal BBC machine would break up. I assumed that he felt he had little time and must take risks; he wasn't there to rearrange the deck–chairs. But neither was he there to rush about aimlessly. His brain sat coolly in the middle of the frenetic activity, observing, collating, analysing, making judgements and forcing decisions.

There were several stages to my discovery of this brain. The first was the quality of the letters he wrote defending *Thought for the Day* on Radio Scotland. Some managers and news editors got jittery if the overlap between this "religious slot" and the news content of the *Good Morning Scotland* sequence in which it was set involved comment which was thought too overtly political. This nervousness was accentuated when MPs wrote to the controller with specific objections. I recall a then junior MP, Michael Forsyth, as being a dab hand at seeing achilles heels in a *Thought for the Day* script and registering a complaint. Alastair's replies were cool and unrepentant.

Unlike some managers he had a keen sense of the role of the Kirk in Scottish history involving centuries of overlap of Kirk and state, religion and politics. The *Guardian* under his editorship had an exceptional record for a UK broadsheet of covering the General Assembly. He wasn't going to be the one to downgrade the independence of Kirk ministers on air: and he said so, in letters which were models of pith. His main point was usually that he saw no point in asking people to come in and say what they thought and then censoring them. This was a typical Hetherington thrust; depending on your perspective, it either brilliantly grasped the only point that mattered; or it missed the point entirely. To the pressurised departmental editor, either in religion or news, it could look like selling the editorial pass, for producers spent much time curtailing the excesses of some contributors in order to achieve an acceptable balance. But I always gave two and three-quarter cheers when I read one of these elegant put-downs to pomposity; one could only admire the chutzpah.

Decades of honing editorials had made his use of English a class act. To compare such missives with present–day faxes and e–mails would suggest a gap not between planets but galaxies.

My next encounter with the Hetherington brain was more direct. By the end of a year, I could see that certain areas like news, documentaries and network drama were getting priority attention for staff and resources. They were getting them directly from Alastair who would buck the usual channels for resource decisions. But others, including religion, were going dutifully through the system. The system had actually been dealing with religion rather favourably, and we were steadily expanding our range of programmes, especially on television. But I saw certain areas now gaining resource advantage. So I went to my line manager, Pat Walker, head of programmes, who in the interregnum had been acting controller. Pat was not a systems man in the sense of being rigid. He was an unusually creative and sensitive boss who over the years had been a shrewd spotter of talent, seeing growing points and nurturing them with managerial craftiness and pastoral care. But his style was quiet and ironic: he was a connoisseur's manager. Being a BBC man through and through, he saw his role as keeping essential systems and processes – and people – going in the midst of the Hetherington turbulence. When I asked him if I should now deal with the controller directly for resources, Pat, always a realist, said yes.

It was the sheer un–BBCness of the subsequent encounter that gobsmacked me. I put my case for more resources, especially in film and staff, for opt-out religious programmes. Alastair listened. That was formidable enough: his brain had turned full force on me, like a lighthouse beam arrested at an angle. He asked a few questions. Then he said, in his quick, light voice, "I've taken that on board. What exactly do you want?" I told him. "Right, you'll have it." Within a few weeks we did.

From then on, he took an intense interest in the content of our programmes, and every significant boat we pushed out seemed to receive his vigorous approval. He can't possibly have liked all the programmes, but he saw what I was aiming at. Protecting my right to take risks led to an illuminating confrontation with the Scottish religious advisory committee, a quango of mainly church people who met twice a year, viewed programmes, lunched, quaffed, and retrospectively assessed output. By the time Alastair arrived, I'd managed to broaden its membership, but once the meeting registered serious unhappiness about a new TV studio series, *The Yes, No, Don't Know Show.* The format is now *de rigeur,* but I believe we were the first in Britain to attempt it. Kenneth Roy leapt around the audience as Kilroy does, and an audience voted on ethical and theological questions. What would now be regarded as merely lively audience participation was then seen by theologians, church dignitaries, and some BBC traditionalists as unstructured chaos likely to lead to the end of civilisation as we know it. Most of the committee registered dismay.

At which point Alastair breezed into the room. With his disarming boy scout smile, he held up the ratings figures. The audiences were unprecedentedly huge, and growing. "Are you saying all those people are wrong?", he asked the churchmen.

As with *Thought for the Day,* he was either grasping the only point that mattered, or if you believe formal theological dialogue to be the *sine qua non* of religious discussion, he was missing it. I gave three and three quarter cheers; and the committee dispersed to its book–lined studies baffled as to how Alastair, by an apparent sleight of hand, had so easily turned the tables on them. It was simple enough: Hetherington, the innocent, had asked about the emperor's clothes.

This was a controller who loved debate. His treatment of the Broadcasting Council for Scotland was more respectful than his routing of the religious advisory committee. The BCS was BBC Scotland's governing body, and Alastair saw it as his praetorian guard against London. But he had a more intriguing vision of its potential value: it could be a debating chamber for ideas and a forcing house for policy change. Again, he was either brilliantly right, or, in BBC terms, exactly wrong, for there was a danger of stepping over the line of the editorial independence of producers, guarded jealously throughout the BBC's history. I can only speak of how I found it. I was invited to the Broadcasting Council on a couple of occasions to participate in a debate about religious broadcasting. Amazingly, it was a debate with teeth. Instead of religion being discussed cursorily at the end of the meeting, attracting a few bromides or tangential gripes, Alastair launched an hour's disputation which turned into one of the best arguments about religion I've ever heard. At opposite ends of the table were the traditional Christian and distinguished educator, Farquhar Macintosh, and the equally eloquent agnostic sociologist Kay Carmichael. No holds were barred and everyone, including myself, joined in the scrap. Alastair obviously relished it as I did. Instead of leaving under the impression I'd been patronised as a marginal operator, I went back to my work re-energised. That scenario alone is enough to explain why when Alastair left Queen Margaret Drive I felt bereaved. The support he had given was maintained in a general way by others, but the sense that tomorrow, or this afternoon, or in the next ten minutes, something interestingly unexpected might happen had gone; the head of steam in the creative boiler was dissipated.

I suppose it was all bound to end in tears, especially after the fiasco of the negative referendum result. After that there was no reason for London to support a Scottish risk-taker. And the experiment did contain a built-in contradiction. Alastair believed in collegiate debate under inspirational leadership. He arranged many evening suppers and dinners at Queen Margaret Drive where colleagues and guests could thrash out ideas; almost as if BBC Scotland was an independent college. But in reality, it was no college. Still less was it a university. It was a local campus, controlled by a remote university senate in London.

On that campus, programme makers ran individual fiefdoms within a complex managerial and technical structure. The Hetherington attempt to single-handedly remodel that structure was heroic. And it was heroism, not heroics; he was in deadly earnest. Such single-mindedness can involve broken bones, hurt egos, and large mistakes. Revolution is more painful than evolution. But I, and others of my peers, found Alastair's commitment inspirational. The approach may at times have been managerially defective, but it was intellectually serious. And an additional component should be recognised. There was a passion in his intensity which revealed itself towards the end of his regime; he began to make his own films, climbing mountains. Some found this irritating, because he was taking resources and the best film-making talent from other programme-makers; but I thought it moving. He was a genuine mountain person, and the concepts were imaginative. He was patronised by some TV cognescenti as if he was a one-dimensional journalist. When he discussed with me the image-centred filming we were developing, it was perfectly obvious that he had a keen sense of visual metaphor as a conduit to reality. To him, in fact, reality was many-sided. As he showed when he elected to follow his controllership by running the Inverness radio station and doing some model pieces of radio journalism, he never lost the passion to get to the centre of reality, to understand, but also to do. In him, mind, spirit, and action were synonymous.

What a pity that first devolution referendum didn't work. Then the Glasgow BBC might have developed beyond a branch–line operation, and Alastair might have realised his dream.

Well, it was interesting. It's not every day that a Scot gets the chance to take a great British institution head-on. Alastair did it twice. He made of the *Guardian* a triumphant success. He made of the BBC a heroic... no, I can't say failure. Certainly, religious programmes benefited, as did many others.

All in all, it was a historic event I wouldn't have missed. I'll always be grateful to Alastair for my sharing in his bravehearted exploration of heightened self-belief, intellectual ebullience, and risky freedom. Why did he climb the BBC mountain? Because it was there.

What was his game?

Thomas Prag

My first acquaintance with Inverness was being seconded to help set up Radio Highland for the BBC in 1976. Like many, I fell in love and took the first chance to go back, particularly since the manager was Bill Carrocher, with whom I had got on so well. When he appointed me his number two in 1978 I was looking forward to several years having fun working with Bill. But the controller of BBC Scotland, one Alastair Hetherington, had plans for Bill – which were to give Alastair himself a wee twist in his career. I only knew him by his considerable reputation as a newspaper Olympian at the *Guardian*. I probably expected to meet him a few times in his exalted role as the head of auntie in Glasgow, but I certainly didn't expect to get to know him well or work with him.

In our Highland fastness we were aware that this man was something special. We were also aware that he was not a man to play the BBC by its unwritten rules (or even its written ones) and he was getting himself into trouble with London. Since he was doing so largely because he thought Scotland knew best how to run its broadcasting affairs, we thought that on the whole he was probably a good thing. He was clearly committed to the development of the BBC outposts like Inverness and the islands – another plus. But would he win the war? Rumour in the BBC spun faster than a 78 and it didn't sound good: AH needed some trusted troops around him. The charismatic Bill Carrocher knew Scotland and its politics well and had been a professional diplomat in the Commonwealth Office. Perhaps most importantly he, like Alastair, was not a career BBC man. So it wasn't too surprising that Bill was drafted into Glasgow to watch Alastair's back – too late, as it turned out. The damage was done and the DG had had enough of the maverick. Summoned to London, he was told that he would have to leave the job they had persuaded him so hard to take in the first place, but they offered him a posh posting to New York if he wanted it. The top brasses' jaws fell when Alastair turned down New York. but as the manager's job at BBC Highland was vacant, could he go there please? They couldn't think of an answer.

We were somewhat gobsmacked in Inverness too! Why on earth did this great editor and journalist want to exile himself to the Highlands? We trembled at the prospect, but having lost "our" Bill (pinched by AH in the first place) it was a relief to have someone we could look up to, and not be stuck with a BBC young turk using Inverness as a notch on his cv.

We got to know each other pretty quickly. The story goes that in his first week he asked his secretary Mary Ann (a Gaelic speaker inherited from Bill) to bring in a copy of the *New Statesman*. "Surely," came the reply. The only problem being that she didn't know what he was talking about. Dashing down to the control room she enlisted the help of chief engineer Alan (Lord) Robbins, who was known to be up on these things. He suggested that if she was quick (and lucky) she might find a copy at Hetty's, the local wee shoppie that stocked everything from pork pies to pornography. He also suggested that while she was at it she could try and get a *Spectator* too. By now, Alastair was suffering withdrawal symptoms and couldn't understand why it was taking so long to find a copy or why she wasn't in her office when he went to check. Hetty's didn't let her down and, catching her breath, she delivered the desired periodical to his desk – and before he could comment on the delay added: "... and would you like a *Spectator* too?" Our bill at the newsagents doubled from then on.

But why *was* he behind a very modest desk in Inverness

instead of writing his memoirs or taking up a glamorous job in the big city? Was it some kind of joke? Were we to be part of his revenge on the BBC? Perhaps he wanted to try out some new theories on us. The real answers became obvious soon enough.

He was closer to those hills that demanded his attention and the wide open spaces that let him breathe – and the odd round of golf was an attraction too. But the less obvious reason was that he wanted to learn – to get back to the roots of his profession. He wanted to be a radio reporter – and he wanted us to teach him.

Far from being the remote chief in his fastness, he simply wanted to be part of the team and volunteered to be sent off to cover anything and everything. In particular he developed an appetite for local government and became a regular sight at council meetings and committees. What the independently minded Highland councillors made of him isn't recorded – I suspect many hadn't any idea of his illustrious journalistic background and treated him as a rather mature, very bright trainee, who struggled with the technical kit, but always seemed to be one step ahead of them with his questions. Of course there were others who knew who he was only too well and were delighted to exploit his talents for incisiveness and vision. He was soon invited to all the right dinners and smoke-filled rooms and our newsroom suddenly became rather well informed.

But the bread and butter work was from the diary. Whether it was planning, development or education committees, Alastair treated these apparently mundane meetings with enthusiasm and curiosity. He might well come back with some pithy remarks about what he thought of the level of debate, the incredible density of the average councillor's brain and so on, but he covered them as if they were crucial sessions at Westminster. As senior programme man it sometimes fell to me to "produce" his radio pieces. I'm sure I must have been patronising and arrogant, but he didn't seem to mind. He had no trouble in understanding how to make his journalistic skills work on radio, but the "gubbins" (Uher portable recorders and the like) weren't quite so easy.

He went to the Isle of Lewis on one occasion to record something for a network radio feature – probably for Radio 3.

He endured the long ferry journey on a rough day with the precious Uher never leaving his side – proud as punch, the intrepid one-man team brought back the story. The engineers in London weren't impressed with the quality, however, and insisted he did it all again (they never could understand the distances involved). This time he had to take our one and only Nagra (the Rolls Royce of portable recorders) *and* an engineer who knew how to work it.

His career at Radio Highland soon broadened out and he must have done almost every job in the place from presenting *Morning Report* at the crack of dawn to covering royal visits and elections. I'm sure he was tempted, but too polite, to suggest he could probably manage a Gaelic programme too. Meanwhile I had the best of both worlds. I was working with a great editor as my boss – yet he didn't really want to be bothered with running the place, so he let me get on with it.

From his eyrie of a flat at Bunchrew House (then a rather run-down country house – now a smart hotel) he enjoyed a modicum of entertaining. Given his high profile he knew all sorts of important folk who often came up to see him. Some of them had rather mixed feelings, as they tended to be taken out for a "'bit of fresh air". A bit of fresh air meant chasing Alastair as he strode up a wee hill – "wee" being a relative term. Most were left gasping in his wake.

When he left us, he took with him new skills, new friends, new Munros – and a new wife. 1979 was a year of elections and local Tory agent Sheila Cameron gave him an insight into the mysteries of Highland politics. He seemed impressed – and she became the new Mrs H. He got that one right!

Peacock

Tom Nossiter

My wife Jean and I first met Alastair and Sheila in July 1985. Unusually, given that friendships are normally formed early in life and that our four backgrounds were superficially very different, it has proved a lasting and precious relationship.

Alastair had been appointed to the Peacock committee on the future of the BBC. Professor Blumler, director of the centre for television research at Leeds University, and I had bid for the contract to conduct an international survey of how different systems of paying for television affected what the viewer had on offer.

We were on holiday in Scotland. Time was pressing, so it was arranged that we would drive down from Loch Awe to be met by Alastair off the ferry at Brodick on Arran. It was the only (half) day in a fortnight when the clouds parted. The view from High Corrie was stunning; Sheila's Scottish tea fulfilling. Only one thing nonplussed me. At 4.30 Alastair popped outside and announced: "The boat's on time: we'd better go." (I learned later that Alastair's time-keeping is legendary.)

When our contract was completed, and walking and talking began, I asked Alastair why we had got the job. His answer was Scots laconic: you were the cheapest.

In a very real sense, Jean and I knew Alastair, or more exactly what he stood for, long before we ever met. We were from skilled northern working class backgrounds and the *Manchester Guardian* was our parish magazine. Meeting Alastair was especially poignant: we shared Suez. His courage in putting the paper he deeply loved and his own career on the line is well recorded though no less remarkable for re-reading.

I was a bit part player in the last spasms of Empire. By chance I came off the parade ground at Catterick, having completed my basic national service training at 0800 hours on October 4, 1956. The officer in charge casually announced "we" had invaded Suez and that we were on standby. As a raw eighteen-year-old, marking time before going to university, being shot didn't cross my mind, but the cause did. Whether by design or default, the only broadsheet paper taken on the camp was the *Times*, but exposure as a sixth former to Alastair Hetherington's editorials as foreign and defence editor of the *Manchester Guardian* had inured me to jingoism. Push did not come to shove – the adventure was over as quickly as the proverbial Naafi break.

One of Alastair's angularities is that he is not a dinner party person. Of course, he is faultless on such occasions, but those who have got to know him well realise he is not fully at ease. He is far from solemn, but he wants real conversation with real people of whatever background. His table is monastic: a baron of beef, vegetables of the season and a modest, well-chosen libation laced with genuine exchange. Home and away he insists on washing up.

Alastair was visiting. Soon after returning from a walk with the dogs, Jean's father arrived. Like Alastair he is a big man. Though not formally educated, Irvin is well read and deeply anti-establishment. Millstone grit and granite proceeded to exchange war stories and then analyse campaigns. Grandad meeting Gruaniad was a classic engagement. They still ask after each other with warmth. Irvin will look up from the *Guardian* crossword and ask: "And how is Alastair?"

In civilian life, Alastair had had three distinct careers: press, broadcasting and university, but there is an essential consistency throughout, centred on a respect for a civilised and civilising society. What makes him exceptionally loveable is that this commitment spills over into his personal life. Great man he is, but unlike many in public life he never condescends. He not only affects to be interested in ordinary folk: he simply is.

I was mentioning this appreciation to a friend who had worked as a young sub on the *Guardian* many years ago. His memory was vivid. Handing over the style book, Alastair had said: "Remember the *Guardian* is read by literate people." Then a pause. "'Beauty spots' are out," he added. "That's sloppy. Go and find out why it's beautiful and evoke it in language precisely." Alastair's TV series on great walks and the two little booklets on Arran walks do just that.

Alastair is a great respecter of the elements, natural and political. He is rarely taken unawares. Those who have had the privilege of staying with Alastair and Sheila on Arran know the ritual of Scots caution. The weather forecast has been digested. Then he goes into the garden on the 100-metre ice-age cliff and sniffs the air. Next he surveys the Sound and turns to inspect the cloud round Goat Fell. Finally he opines whether it is to be a short or a long one (walk not whisky). Even on the potter, he never departs without his fellwalker's survival kit.

Because of his peripatetic lifestyle, he has never owned a dog. Being Alastair, he makes do with borrowing his friends' dogs. One day we set off for North Arran – a long one – with the objective of seeing Harold Macmillan's ancestral croft. Caught at the summit of the ridge by a sudden squall we ended in a huddle as bitingly cold stair-rods stabbed us. When the storm had passed over, out came the rations. The for-once cowed young black labrador puppy was served first with Alastair's answer to Kendal Mint Cake: Stilton and marmalade sandwiches.

With political elements, Alastair has demonstrated the same qualities. The strategic objective is unchanging – making communications in an imperfect world serve citizens rather than consumers or their greedy corporate manipulators.

He won't approve of a cliché, but his major battles have been won *festina lente*. The decision to bring the *Guardian* out against Suez was brave, but it was carefully calculated. Likewise the decision to preserve the paper he loved by moving it to London. The most difficult of all the battles was whether or not to merge the *Guardian* with the *Times*, a now-forgotten nadir in the paper's struggle for viability.

Which brings me to my own experience of Alastair as a field commander when under his direction, with my Leeds colleagues, we offered commissioned evidence to the Peacock committee.

For good and bad reasons Mrs Thatcher, supported by the brilliant and the brilliantine, had systematically sought to undermine the pillars of the British establishment. The comfortable duopoly of the BBC and ITV with its barely concealed disdain for middle England was exposed. The DG was no Reith. With changing technology, broadcasting was no longer nationally sovereign.

On March 27, 1985, the home secretary (Leon Brittan) announced an enquiry with Professor Alan Peacock as chairman. By May 17 the full committee had been appointed and a year later the report was delivered. Legally, it was the Report of the Committee on Financing the BBC, but Peacock rightly took a broad view of the terms of reference. His team was to look at the putative effects of advertising or sponsorship on the domestic output of the BBC, the likely knock-on effects of any such changes on the media system in Britain and "the identification of a range of options for the introduction, in varying amounts and on different conditions, of advertising or sponsorship on some or all of the BBC's Home Services".

Tucked away in the terms of reference was a pregnant-with possibilities allusion to the impact of such changes on the range and quality of existing broadcasting services. This was Alastair's opportunity.

In the parish politics of the Whitehall village, "letting the viewer decide" was the philosophy of the Department of Trade and Industry while "range and quality" was Home Office code for the defence of public service broadcasting against the high tide of global down-market forces. Were programmes to be no different from anything else in Mr Murdoch's international car boot sale?

Besides the chair, there were six members of the committee: Sam Brittan, elder brother of the home secretary; Judith Chalmers, a travel journalist who presented Thames TV's *Wish you were here?*; Jeremy Hardie, chairman of National Provident and of some local radio stations as well as prospective SDP candidate for Norwich South; Anthony (Lord) Quinton, the philosopher president of Trinity College, Cambridge, and chairman of the British Library; Sir Peter Reynolds, variously Rank Hovis McDougall, Walls, Boots, and Guardian Royal Exchange; and Hetherington himself, then professor of media studies at the University of Stirling.

Major Hetherington was up against it. The key members of the committee were Peacock and Brittan, both formidable exponents of free market principles and consumer sovereignty. Peacock was a senior academic in economics and public finance. He had also been a senior civil servant in the DTI and much else in the policy process. Sam Brittan was a distinguished economist on the *FT*. The other members were in their own fields the great and the good, but unlikely to have the time or expertise to overturn the agenda.

The inclusion of Alastair was interesting. If he was intended to represent the token balance, it was a lapse of judgement. Even more improbable is the claim by one insider at the time that because Sheila had been a Conservative agent, Alastair was malleable. He was, of course, acceptable to Peacock: for all their political differences, they shared a Scottish intellectual background. I fantasise on the *Yes Minister* discussion on the choice of a public service broadcasting totem pole: good war, Royal Commission on the Police, didn't get on with auntie in London when he was controller of BBC Scotland...and so on.

Be that as it may, Alastair's battle plan was clear. Peacock was also of the Scottish enlightenment tradition, a political economist devoid of dogmatism or vanity. The only time I heard Alastair's controlled anger was when he condemned Glasgow University media group's *More Bad News* as "a disgrace to the University of Glasgow". It was only then that I understood the depths of his commitment to intellectual rigour and his Scottishness.

The chairman's agenda-setting paper took account of the anxieties that advertising on the BBC would lead Britain down an American freeway, but there was a note of scepticism in Peacock's "we must seriously question whether America is a realistic model" for UK broadcasting. It was Alastair who took charge of this dimension of the overall enquiry, visiting the United States and most importantly guiding the Leeds' investigation closely. In particular it was his idea that the range of programming should and could be monitored for a week of prime-time in seven countries from the USA via Europe to Australia. Working to tight deadlines, his team at Stirling University provided the data for the tables which categorised the reality of choice. The viewer was best served not by profit-maximising markets nor more or less enlightened governments, but by a "mixed economy" of public and private.

Alastair's contribution to the debate on how the finance of broadcasting affected its quality is less quantifiable but equally real. Blumler and I were enjoined to interview those who made programmes and whose who controlled them, across the board. Was the elusive "quality" simply subjective? Given Alastair's catholicity of taste in viewing, it could not be elitist.

In terms of international awards, British programming of all kinds won far more accolades than all the competition put together, but what were the underlying criteria? Technical excellence was a necessary but not sufficient condition. Blumler provided a devastating critique of the play of free market (so-called) forces in the United States based on the frank accounts of the American industry. I interviewed more than a hundred greatly respected past and present British programme-makers in every department from light entertainment and sport through sit coms to *Jewel in the Crown*.

From quiz shows through serials and soaps to opera, there was a persuasive consensus. The sufficient conditions of quality were innovation (*Yes Minister, Monty Python*) and relevance to the human condition which could as well be *Steptoe and Son* as *Hard Times*. Julia Smith, whose memorial is *EastEnders*, after wryly complaining that Dickens was not alive to write for her, said with absolute sincerity: "Mrs Whitehouse doesn't understand that it is no good preaching moral choice. We are trying ... to make people think about relationships and the problems around us."

The Peacock report remains one of the most formidable investigations of modern British government – and it was completed to time and budget. Change in the structure of British broadcasting was inevitable and desirable, but that advertising, sponsorship or pay-per-view were avoided on BBC television and radio is really down to Alastair. He had the vision to see how simplicities could be refuted empirically.

At the end of the second draft of this tribute to an extraordinary man, I broke off to watch the news. After the moving footage of the funeral of the three boys murdered at Ballymoney, ITV offered its audience the (American) Springer show featuring "the girl who dates convicts". That we are not force-fed this on all channels much of the time is largely Alastair's doing.

An era passes

Philip Schlesinger

More than anyone else, Alastair Hetherington was instrumental in bringing me to Scotland in 1989. I came north of the border to take up the UK's first established chair in film and media studies at Stirling University. It was no small decision for me or for my family. It was one thing to have been a regular and enthusiastic visitor to Scotland over the years and quite another to up sticks and make the country our home.

Alastair was persuasive – nay, stubbornly insistent – that Stirling was the place for me. And so, indeed, it has turned out. He wanted me to build on the foundations that he had laid in his third, and final, career as research professor of media studies. He had set up a small research institute alongside Stirling's well-regarded film and media studies department and was energetically undertaking a series of studies of print and broadcast journalism.

Although Alastair's university years were rather few compared to those he spent in newspapers, they exceeded his five years at the BBC, and he laid down some important foundations at Stirling. Undoubtedly, he felt some pride and satisfaction in attaining the professorial title that had also been his father's and in concluding his writing days as – at least in part – an academic author. Only in part, because in this concluding burst of activity, alongside his research Alastair wrote pieces about Perthshire and the Highlands and Islands, produced occasional journalism, and capped it all with a brief memoir of his time in BBC Scotland.

It was journalism and its study that provided the first common thread of many encounters. But as time passed by, while walking the hills, we talked politics and history, as well as engaging in some more intimate ruminations on the vagaries of life, and that became the stuff of our conversations. Alastair disclosed much of himself on these purposeful wanderings. So rather rapidly after my arrival in Scotland, our initial, cordial, and somewhat professional association transmuted into friendship.

This friendship also came to include our families. Once I had accepted the Stirling chair, I came north with my wife in the sodden gloom of November 1988 to meet colleagues, and then again in the snowy February of 1989 to find a house. Sheila Hetherington opened her home and her heart to us, providing an unexcelled level of thoughtful and caring hospitality. Alastair could not have been more fortunate in his partner. Her devotion to him should not go unsung. Whether in the Hetheringtons' flat at Bridge of Allan or at High Corrie on the Isle of Arran, we have been lucky enough to enjoy the pleasures of the table and good conversation, most commonly after the inevitable walk. These have been moments to treasure and their perfection has owed much to Sheila's gracious disposition.

Alastair will not have recalled our very first encounter and I doubt I ever mentioned it. It contained the seed of our future dialogue. But whoever knows these things at the time? He had come to speak to some of the pioneers of media research in Britain. Gathered together as the mass communications study group of the British Sociological Association, a small, at that time decidedly unfashionable, community of twenty or so academics would meet in the rather cheerless seminar rooms of the Polytechnic of Central London at Regent Street and later on in the even pokier surroundings of the City University.

An aficionado of this little circus in the early 1970s, recently graduated from Oxford, I was a young PhD candidate at the LSE, working on a study of the BBC's news departments that eventually became a book. Alastair was one of a small number of luminaries from the world of journalism prepared to engage in self-critical discussion of their work. He came to speak about being editor of the *Guardian*. He gave a lucid, somewhat austere account of the dilemmas of editing Britain's leading liberal broadsheet, and a rather matter-of-fact description of his dealings with the elite worlds of politics and diplomacy. It was a talk entirely of a piece with the world so splendidly evoked in his durable memoir, *Guardian Years*.

Alastair was direct in answering questions and seemed somehow both affable and distant. But he was not at all unapproachable as he stopped to chat to some of the younger folk at the end of his talk before heading back to his newspaper.

And then I lost sight of him until the early 1980s. Now, beginning to be established as a sociologist in London, I received a letter from Alastair quite out of the blue. He had applied to the Social Science Research Council for a grant to study decision-making in several national newspapers and broadcasting organisations. He was by now based at Stirling University where Sir Kenneth Alexander had invited him to undertake some journalism research. In 1982 he had become research professor there.

I had refereed Alastair's research proposal and suggested some substantial amendments. I recall thinking that there was quite a gulf between how I approached the study of journalism as a social scientist and Professor Hetherington's formulations, which had been clearly influenced by his years of insider experience. I thought he lacked sufficient detachment. These critical comments had no doubt been relayed to Alastair. Whether he knew who had been their author is unclear. At all events, he wrote requesting a discussion with me.

We met for lunch one day in 1982 at one of his clubs, the Athenaeum, an anthropologically rich moment for me, at any rate, as I absorbed the atmosphere of this slice of establishment life. It was a pleasant and relaxed occasion. After rather fulsome praise for my book on the BBC, Alastair told me it showed that sociologists could indeed understand journalism and not just denounce it. This was a time when relations between some academic critics of journalism and many media professionals –

especially in broadcasting – were at their worst. He asked me to act as a consultant for the study that was to become *News, Newspapers and Television.* Over a period of two years, 1983-84, Alastair would send draft chapters to me for comment and from time to time we would meet up in London to discuss the work. He was always politely receptive to my observations, but did not always agree with them.

Then, in May 1985, came Alastair's appointment to the Peacock committee on financing the BBC. To my eyes, he was a frenetic member of the shuttling classes, for ever flying between Scotland and London on public business. This continued a pattern set when he had been controller of BBC Scotland from 1975 to 1980. He went further afield, too, to the USA, France, Germany and Italy, as part of the committee's efforts to learn comparative lessons. Observation of Alastair's itinerary brought home to me Scotland's peripherality in relation to the centres of power and decision-making. Now for the past decade, regularly London-bound, I too have had ample opportunity to turn theory into practice.

While generally very guarded about the committee's deliberations, Alastair did make it clear that he was unhappy with what he saw as the increasing threat of market principles to public service broadcasting. He was one of the committee's traditionalist wing at a time when this was out of keeping with the dominant view. The Peacock committee's report was unquestionably a landmark intervention in public debate and in shaping media policy. It marked a sea-change in thinking about broadcasting finance and delivery. Indeed, the changes so presciently anticipated in 1986 will continue to unfold after the millennium. Whatever Alastair's ultimate reservations may have been about the quite radical re-regulation of broadcasting that followed on from Peacock, he was to be indelibly associated with the United Kingdom's most seminal report on the subject.

At around this time, our relationship moved onto a new plane. Alastair and I met once again in the Athenaeum in early 1985, this time for tea and a conversation conducted *sotto voce.* The previous year, Alastair had become chairman of the Scott Trust, the unique body that owns the Guardian Media Group. Unlike any other proprietor, the trust ensures that profits are reinvested in the company and not distributed as dividends, as there are no shareholders to please. The trustees had for some time wanted to publicise the trust's workings and to bring to public attention the fact that a newspaper group could function without being the plaything of a media mogul. Moreover, as the trust arrangements had long permitted a loss-making newspaper, the *Guardian*, to survive by virtue of cross-subsidy within the company, there was a second message about how to sustain a diversity of opinion in the press.

Alastair asked me whether I would write a short pamphlet on the Scott Trust to mark its fiftieth anniversary. I would be given unimpeded access to the Scott Trust's minutes and be able to interview any trustees that I wished. It was for me to write as I found.

Thinking back on this conversation, and others, what I recall is Alastair's depth of commitment to the Scott Trust and the *Guardian*, his deep love for the newspaper and his enduring gratitude to the imaginative and self-denying gesture that had led to the trust's foundation in the mid-1930s. Even a decade after relinquishing the paper's editorship, Alastair plainly remained a *Guardian* man through and through, fiercely proud of the permissive arrangements that had allowed him to flourish as an outstanding editor, one who had saved the paper for a secure future and who had laid the foundations for its exceptional contemporary reputation. For me, being trusted to write about the trust was one of the greatest compliments Alastair could have bestowed. My respect and liking for the man grew as I came to know him better in this period. He became an occasional visitor to the family home, charming my wife and young daughters with his cordiality.

After a period of research, the pamphlet was eventually published in summer 1986, and Alastair, true to his word, had left this writer to his own devices, though we politely haggled over a phrase or two. He resigned – with manifest regret – from the chairmanship of the trust, in accordance with that body's rules, when he reached the age of seventy. He would often speak of the trust afterwards, somewhat wistfully, and monitor the *Guardian's* reportage with a keen eye. Undoubtedly, he felt that with his departure an era of informality and gentlemanly understandings had truly passed and that the trust had become a much more professional body, more akin to a company's main board, the trustees acting increasingly like directors. To some extent he was right, for as my own follow-up research on the Scott Trust demonstrated, the trustees' self-understanding of their role and their practices had indeed shifted.

Alastair retired from Stirling, after putting the final touches to his study of the televising of parliament, *Cameras in the Commons*. He was thrilled when the university honoured him with an emeritus professorship. Satisfied that the department was about to set a new course, Alastair very much wanted to take a back seat. We held a dinner to mark his retirement and, amid a welter of affectionate tributes, presented him with the handsome fountain pen and pencil set which, typically through Sheila, we had eventually discovered was what he really wanted. Alastair's speech was brief, witty and self-disparaging.

But that was a year after I had taken up the new chair. Once I had been installed, Alastair would offer advice – but with great punctiliousness and only when asked. He still supported the department's work and was an opening speaker at our first media management forum in 1990, a closed seminar held at Stirling that attracted the principal movers and shakers of the broadcasting world and key figures from the wider policy community. Moreover, due to our close connections with academic colleagues in Catalonia, Alastair was invited to judge an international journalism competition in Barcelona during the 1992 Olympics.

But for him – such occasional forays aside – retirement really meant drawing the line. He observed the film and media studies department's rapid growth in size and its rising international reputation in research and teaching with benign interest, still keeping in touch with some of the founding group. Yet, over the years, Alastair's became more and more of a fleeting presence in J corridor of the Pathfoot Building. His great passion for walking certainly absorbed much of his time, and when possible I would tag along, joining him, and occasionally others, in the Southern Highlands, on his beloved Arran or in the Ochils. We would meet up maybe three or four times a year over several years, walking in all weathers. At well over seventy, his great agility and intimate knowledge of Scotland's hills and mountains compelled my admiration.

By 1991 Alastair was clearly determined to settle his accounts with the past. He wrote a memoir of his time as controller, BBC Scotland, a professionally trying period for him. Re-reading it now, one can readily see that *Inside BBC Scotland* is a continuation, albeit in a minor key, of *Guardian Years*. It is the short second volume of Alastair's professional autobiography. But much more than that, it remains an illuminating text for those thinking about the problems of devolved public service broadcasting in an autonomous Scotland, a matter of great political sensitivity today, with elections to the devolved Edinburgh parliament soon to come.

Alastair Hetherington has much of which to be proud. Unquestionably, he is best known in Britain and abroad for his time as editor of the *Guardian*. In Scotland, there is also the public profile he gained by his tenure of the hot seat at Queen Margaret Drive. His achievements in these posts massively overshadow the distinct success of his third and final career at Stirling University. But that does not mean that Alastair Hetherington's contribution to the formation of media research in Scotland should go unremarked, nor has it.

Media, Marxism, and marmalade

C. Kay Weaver

When I first met Alastair Hetherington he was fast approaching his seventieth birthday and the emeritus research professor in the department of film and media studies at Stirling University, where I was studying for a BA. I was in my early twenties at that time and I like to think it was because of the age gap between us that I had no idea why Alastair held this professorship, let alone what it meant. In the context of what and where I was studying, however, that sounds like a rather lame excuse for my blatant ignorance of the British media and one of its highly respected journalists and long-standing editors. Fortunately though, Alastair – who has always struck me as mostly interested in helping others acquire and better their knowledge – was not intent on identifying my limitations when we met. Instead, he offered me a job as a research assistant conducting content analyses of regional newspaper and television news reporting for his study *News in the Regions*.

The aim of this project was to investigate the public service performance of the regional news media in England and Scotland, chiefly drawing from Alastair's numerous interviews with journalists and editors. My ancillary role involved quantifying which news events were reported in the regional media and the significance attributed to these in terms of air time or column space. This was a simple enough task in itself, but it came with an unexpected education – one which Alastair sought to provide to as wide an audience as possible – in the sometimes volatile relationship between media theory and research and media practice.

It was one day during the early stages of this project that I, freshly imbued with Marxist media criticism from my undergraduate studies, began extolling the virtues of an ideological examination of the news priorities of the regional media, and suggested that Alastair ask the journalists about their "ideological agendas". I very quickly learnt that words such as "ideology", "encoded meanings" and "myth" are a red rag of jargon to Alastair. He has little patience for abstract theorising, which characterises journalistic practice as upholding the power and authority of the rich and privileged.

Had I read Alastair's earlier work, *News, Newspapers and Television*, I might have anticipated his somewhat cynical view of certain aspects of academic media criticism. There, he pointedly rejects several seminal sociological theories of news reporting and argues for a more pragmatic appreciation of journalist production. This is not to say that Alastair dismisses media theory altogether. Rather, he perceives no common ground between those who work to produce the news, and those who engage in that very particular brand of Marxist media criticism which was so popular in the 1970s and 1980s. In his view:

> There is ... a gulf between the way journalists look at their work and the way sociologists see it. That is unfortunate for both, for if sociologists were to write in plainer language, and if journalists were less distrustful of sociologists, both sides would benefit. The rift is widened by conflicting use of words, by what may seem to journalists tortuous explanations of simple procedures, and by the Marxist background of some sociological studies.

Given that my own views of the media had been shaped by precisely these Marxist sociological studies, I imagine that to Alastair I must have somewhat resembled the young man described in the "Personal Postscript" to *News, Newspapers and Television*, where he remarks:

> While the last part of this book was being written, a student from a reputable polytechnic came to consult me. He had been thinking of a career in journalism but had concluded that newspaper journalists were corrupted by commercial ownership and broadcasters too much influenced by the government of the day. He was intelligent, and his words made me wonder what sort of teaching he had had and how much time he had spent reading newspapers, listening to radio news or watching television news.

As this suggests, Alastair believes that the most balanced and accurate understanding of the media can be achieved through an engagement with its output, rather than purely through the teachings and speculative pronouncements of academic media criticism. This belief is evident in Alastair's research methodology, which situates his work firmly within the tradition of media production analysis.

Clearly, this focus on the processes and imperatives of media production accounts for much of the difficulty Alastair faced in gaining acceptance for *News, Newspapers and Television* and *News in the Regions*, both of which can be characterised as an insider's defence of the profession of journalism and, therefore, as somewhat conservative in their outlook. Yet as investigations of news production practice, their significance should not be dismissed. Both were, after all, conducted before many other media scholars adopted this methodological focus. Indeed, in the context of Boyd-Barrett's statement on current trends in media research, Alastair can perhaps be considered something of a pioneer:

> There is a clear trend in 1990s production research away from the application of formal or abstract frameworks or abstract frameworks toward greater emphasis, through ethnographic method, on the perceptions of the participants themselves. This goes along with a reluctance to analyse the world through the ready-made categories of traditional

sociological empiricism.

Alastair's response to this shift would surely be a characteristic rising of arms in the air accompanied by a jubilant "Hooray!"

Re-reading the books that Alastair published during his time at Stirling, it seems he has on occasion poked considerable fun at abstract media criticism, even though his professorship brought a formal association with this field of inquiry. For example, in response to Galtung and Ruge's formulation of news values derived from cross-national analysis, Alastair outlines his own schema for the codifying of news priorities, drawn from his "instinct about the factors likely to influence news editors, night editors and the editors themselves". The decision to name this schema the "seismic scale" must have been made with tongue firmly in cheek. However, Alastair's claim to have drawn this up from "instinct" also evidences a resistance to the notion that "common sense assumptions" and the often-cited journalistic "gut reaction" for a good story are in need of critical analysis. Characteristically, in defending journalists against the assertion that such assumptions and "gut feelings" are subject to political and institutional bias, Alastair once again appeals to pragmatism:

> Is there bias? Only the usual "socio-centralism" – which is to say the tendency in the media to reinforce the established society, uphold law and order, and accept social reform only gradually. Newspapers and broadcasters usually reflect what they perceive as the attitudes of their readers and audiences; and since most people want peaceful, prosperous and orderly lives, events such as riots and strikes are unpopular.

Articulated here is an obvious rebuking of neo-Marxist media theory, which asserts that the news media support the interests of capital over and above the democratic interests of a well-informed electorate. For Alastair, such "conspiracy theories" contribute nothing toward the development of a dialogue between media institutions and those academic institutions which profess to educate students about the social functions of the media through various media studies degrees. By demonstrating how news producers function on a day-to-day basis and according to the constraints of deadlines and audience expectations, Alastair's publications sought to promote exactly this dialogue. Yet simultaneously, as was the intention, they provided those hoping to pursue a career in journalism with a sense of what their chosen vocation would entail.

Alastair's attempt to open up channels of communication between media institutions and educational establishments was, however, considerably frustrated by the apparent unwillingness of commercial publishers to support his enterprise. He was greatly saddened by his inability to persuade Macmillan that a market did indeed exist for a second edition of *News, Newspapers and Television*. Having failed to convince them through more official means, Alastair attempted to single-handedly bolster demand for its re-publication. One day he entered our office with a university bookshop bag in his hand. When I asked him what he had found to read, I was surprised to discover that he had bought his own *News, Newspapers and Television*. Thinking he must have intended this as a present for someone, or that he must have lost his own copy, I reminded Alastair that there was a small pile of these books in the office cupboard. It was then he explained he was simply trying to keep the sales up so as to force Macmillan to rethink their position. It would perhaps hearten Alastair to know that, though this book never was reprinted, *News, Newspapers and Television* can now be purchased in cyberspace via Macmillan's internet bookshop (http://www.macmillan-press.co.uk/catalogue/0386/0-333-386...)

With the completion of the *News in the Regions* project came a break in the work which Alastair and I did together. During that period, largely through Alastair's introductions, I secured a short internship with *Scotland on Sunday*, while he became absorbed in planning a new opportunity to examine media coverage of matters of both civil and national importance. This came in the shape of the experimental introduction of television cameras into the House of Commons in November 1989. Alastair was commissioned by the Hansard Society to study and report on this new initiative, and – by now a dab hand at using a 12 inch ruler to measure newspaper reporting, and a stop watch to time television news items – I was again invited on board.

My role in this second project was to quantify print and broadcast coverage of events in the House of Commons during the television experiment. As was the case with *News in the Regions*, this content analysis was to provide data on the reports made available to news readers and viewers, while Alastair went out into the field to interview those who wrote and produced these reports. His task was to assess the journalistic perspective on the advantages and disadvantages of *Cameras in the Commons*, as he would later name the short book we compiled from the study.

Once again, I found that embarking on a project with Alastair necessitated some learning on my part. On this occasion, however, it was not journalistic practice which Alastair wanted me to reconsider in relation to what I thought I knew, and what I had learned from secondary resources. Instead, he set to work on providing some schooling in the working of British parliamentary democracy. In this instance, the educational journey was to be a very literal one: Alastair wanted me to spend some time sitting in the gallery of the Commons observing the House in action for myself, and presented me with a plane ticket to London to go and do just that. This gesture not only illustrates the generosity with which Alastair treated an assistant, but also his shrewd belief in the need to gain as complete a picture of a situation as possible in order to evaluate it better.

The central question of the *Cameras in the Commons* study was "Has the televising increased public interest and understanding of Commons affairs?" Whilst this focus was prescribed by the parliamentary select committee on televising of proceedings of the House, it also demonstrates a core concern of Alastair's: that of encouraging consideration of the media's contribution to a civil and democratic society. Alastair was certain that the televising of parliamentary proceedings was a significant and progressive move. For him this represented "a fresh dimension, both in British political life and in broadcasting – a boost for parliament, good for the electorate, and good for television". Undoubtedly, the televising of the House would have continued even if our own study had drawn less optimistic conclusions – the Commons feed very quickly became routinised into television news reporting, and there was no going back from that point. But there is also no denying that Alastair felt extremely proud to be part of this progressive initiative aimed at further opening up British parliamentary democracy to public scrutiny.

There is also an ironic twist to this story in terms of how the *Cameras in the Commons* study was reported by one news organ, given Alastair's earlier castigation of abstract sociological analyses of the news media. On this occasion the boot was on the other foot and Alastair and myself were cast as quantitative academic researchers gone mad in this brief report from the *Scotsman*:

> Alastair Hetherington, the professor of media studies at Stirling University, and Kay Weaver, a research assistant at the university, must have had some boring days in preparing their booklet, *Cameras in the Commons.*
> The two compare in detail television's coverage of parliament with that of the press. Looking at one week, they get their calculators and measuring tapes out. Result: Commons items in the *Guardian* 35, *Times* 51, *Daily Mail* 6, *Sun* 2 and the *Scotsman* 28.
> They then calculate the number of square centimetres of parliamentary coverage with the *Guardian* at 3,513, the *Times* 6,123, the *Daily Mail* 1,062, the *Sun* 207 and the *Scotsman* 3,892.
> Having done that, they measure the total number of square centimetres of direct quotes.

It was a very perceptive jibe, though I can't agree with its description of our job as "boring".

After the *Cameras in the Commons* study, Alastair and I followed our own separate paths of writing and research. He went on to compile an autobiography of his time at BBC Scotland, while I stayed with the department of film and media studies at Stirling, initially involved in a Broadcasting Standards Council research project before moving on to study for a PhD. We remained in contact, though, occasionally getting together for a day's walking in the Scottish mountains, where Alastair guided me up a number of magnificent Munros. During these often-glorious days he would talk of his time with the *Guardian* and about the highs and lows of his position as controller of BBC Scotland. One particular tale I shall always remember being told – with a mischievous glint in his eye as we ascended Ben Cleuch in the Ochils – illustrates Alastair's passionate support for the Scottish media and the frustration which he felt with London's dominance in broadcasting. He recounts this story in *Inside BBC Scotland* in the following words:

> The transfer of Radio 4 from medium to long wave ... I was told in London, meant that even if the Scottish Nationalists became dominant north of the Border, the BBC's Radio 4 would continue to broadcast to the whole of Scotland uninterrupted. When I was back in Glasgow I was quietly informed by a colleague that if a Scottish Assembly was set up and if the Scottish Government wanted a change, the two long transmitters could be altered within half an hour and other outlets given to Radio 4. 'If you give the instruction', I was told,'we shall do it'.

Alastair was clearly thrilled by the idea that a simple turn of a screwdriver could establish a separate broadcasting identity for Scotland. With this I discovered that he was more of a rebel than I had ever given him credit for.

The last time I saw Alastair was on Arran, when we climbed his much loved Goat Fell and descended for a final tea with his wife Sheila before they put me back on my ferry to Ardrossan. It was a sad departure, as I knew that it would be a very long time before I would see either Alastair or Sheila again. As the boat left the terminal I strained to watch their car drive back round the coastal road toward High Corrie. After I lost sight of them in the distance I turned my thoughts to the three days I had left in Scotland before flying out to New Zealand and a lectureship in film and television studies at the University of Waikato. It is a job which I would never have secured had it not been for Alastair providing me with the foundation stones for an academic career. And while I do teach Marxist theories of the media, I also advocate the importance of grounded research into media production practices. I am also fortunate to have "inherited" many of Alastair's academic texts, and grin every time I open one in search of inspiration to find words like "encoded" circled in pencil with his handwriting exclaiming "jargon!" in the margin.

Finally, there is one other rather delicious item which I learnt about from Alastair – Brie and marmalade sandwiches. They are a wonderful treat when you have climbed to the top of a mountain and sit perusing the land stretching out to far horizons below. They taste just as good on a rainy day when clouds hang heavy in the air.

Friendship, love, and truth

Ken and Angela Alexander

Even before we first met Alastair we had a high regard for him. The reasons for this are fairly obvious. The editorship of the *Guardian,* and its policy stances on the major issues of the 1960s and '70s; his decision prior to the Scottish referendum in 1979 to move back to Scotland to participate in the expected "home rule" situation; his period of training and experiences with the BBC in London to prepare himself for a shift of media; his appointment as the BBC chief in Scotland. Here was a man of great talent and a clear set of values which determined what he wanted to do and where he wanted to do it. On top of this, amongst academics at least, the name Hetherington carried its own esteem, with Alastair's father Sir Hector Hetherington, principal of the University of Glasgow for a quarter of a century and recognised as the most experienced and respected vice-chancellor in the Commonwealth. The strength of this esteem may be measured by the fact that although Sir Hector had retired in 1961 and died in 1965, to many in Scotland in the late 1970s Alastair was welcomed back as Sir Hector's son. It should be said that Alastair recognised the sincerity of this and was not at all upset by it; the famous father syndrome is not a part of his psyche.

A matter relating to his father illustrates one of Alastair's strongest characteristics – an ability to lay aside established views and even filial loyalty when faced by a compelling argument which reaches a conclusion different from his own. Sir Charles Illingworth's *University Statesman* deals with the disagreements between the University of Glasgow and the Glasgow Royal Technical College (University of Strathclyde since 1964). Illingworth calls the College proposals "supremely logical and academically impeccable", and argues that "Hetherington should not have allowed himself to be drawn into the controversy; and having become enmeshed, should have become more adroit at escaping". In his foreword referring to this issue Alastair writes ".. some of those who were directly involved now feel the text to be, if anything, too critical of Hector Hetherington's conduct. Having no direct knowledge, I cannot say: I am glad to accept Sir Charles's version as having fairly taken account of conflicting evidence."

A personal comment would be that Sir Hector's expression of opposition to the college and to Strathclyde was civilised and restrained, comparing favourably with that of Sir James Irvine of St Andrews who, speaking at the installation of Lord Todd as first chancellor of Strathclyde said: "I fear we are close to a time at which every garage mechanic will have to have a university degree." From the other side of the argument we much prefer the point made to Ken by the late Sir Samuel Curran, first principal of Strathclyde: "You know, I think that the most important thing we may achieve here is to improve the University of Glasgow."

Alastair's period in charge of the BBC in Scotland was eventful but cut short. His enthusiasm for the concept of devolution and for increasing "regional" control produced tensions with London, personalised as a conflict of philosophies between two Scots – the director general, Alasdair Milne, and Alastair. With an unyielding commitment to their respective views on both sides of this argument it was inevitable that in the end it was Alastair who was sacrificed. But the outcome was unusual, highlighting one of Alastair's most admirable traits – his complete lack of interest in the ranking and status which are inherent in hierarchical organisations. Rather than retire on the basis of whatever compensation would have been provided, he preferred to take control of BBC Highland based in Inverness.

At that time we were living on the Black Isle. With Alastair working in Inverness our friendship took roots, and flourished. This friendship deepened when Alastair married Sheila, a widow whose husband, a highly respected consulting engineer, had been involved in many of the major developments in the Highlands and Islands. Sheila was already a friend, and her youngest daughter and ours were the closest of pals at school, and indeed thereafter. When Alastair retired from the BBC, the Hetheringtons moved to Edinburgh. We moved to Stirling and were able to refresh our friendship with frequent meetings, even more so when the Hetheringtons moved to Bridge of Allan, still the family home. Alastair has a sentimental feel for the Hillfoots, with a grandfather who had owned a pharmacy in Tillicoultry and his father spending his boyhood there and attending Dollar Academy for his schooling.

A redirection of Alastair's experience and talents took place when he was invited to become a professor in the very strong and thriving department of media studies at Stirling University. The student response to the opportunity of hearing – and being able to question – a one-time editor of the *Guardian* and head of the BBC in Scotland was very positive, even enthusiastic. The academic atmosphere, and the opportunities to consult with colleagues, were helpful to Alastair in his new role as a student of the media process, in particular the creation of news programmes for television. For a while a healthy debate developed between researchers at Glasgow University and Alastair at Stirling. At Glasgow the emphasis was on failure of objectivity, even a tendency to pro-establishment bias in news on television, based on analysis of how particular issues were treated. Alastair's approach was quite different, emphasising – as his background encouraged him to – the mechanisms, the nuts and bolts, time constraints etc, of how news programmes had to be produced, and the effect this can have on what is presented – and what is omitted. His statistical analyses did not support the bias argument at all strongly, probably partly because his knowledge and experience made him more sympathetic to the problems and pressures under which newsmen work. The debate died down; we would have liked some attempt to discuss differences and explore whether some joint work could have been undertaken, but academia usually prefers debate to coordinated effort, and current emphasis on research assessment determining resource allocation probably encourages this attitude.

Alastair's research methodology was very detailed and specific. He pursued whatever he thought might have the least bearing on his subject matter. This style was mirrored by his approach to walking and climbing. The shortest route was never on his agenda, and if, *en route,* he saw a hillock or a lochan, then it had to be explored. Even with much less energy it was not at all difficult to keep ahead of Alastair on a walk because he was so determined to see it all. His books on news coverage illustrate this same tendency to incorporate all of what he judges are the relevant factors, very far from the current emphasis in the social sciences on heroic abstraction and even more heroic model building designed to link the key variables in a determinate system. "News rooms are not like that" was Alastair's response to suggestions that he adopt such an approach.

During this period the Hetheringtons and the Alexanders established a company (Scotquest) to make programmes for television. The output was necessarily limited but the quality was good. A series of *Great Walks* for Channel 4 in which young unemployed were the walkers, with plenty of opportunity to make social and other comments, was popular with viewers and much enjoyed in the making by Alastair as producer. The programme which we thought the most impressive was *Columba,* an attempt in fifty five minutes to bring some of the eminence and influence of the man to the viewer. It seemed a pity that this film was not shown again in 1997, fourteen centuries after the death of the saint who established sanctity and scholarship in Iona, and spread these qualities throughout Scotland.

Scotquest made no distinction between programme ideas we thought suitable for BBC or STV. Alastair is entirely free of the cultural snobbery which at one time was exemplified by the attitudes of some senior BBC people to the commercial channels. The phrase "the keelies of Cowcaddens" has been used in our hearing, but no longer, we hope.

One of the most significant contributions Alastair made to the public good arose from his membership of the government committee established to consider the future funding of the BBC. Shortly after the publication of the report (*Financing the BBC*, 1986) a public meeting at Stirling University brought together the chairman of the committee, Sir Alan Peacock, and Alastair. It was clear that Sir Alan regarded Alastair as having been a major influence in limiting the extent of recommended change to considerably less than the chairman would have wished. Somewhat inappropriately, he referred to the presence of the "Kremlin", some measure of the depth of the disagreement which had existed on the committee. Sir Alan was not the first to discover that Alastair's openness of mind was not a sign of weakness of principle but of a determination to hear the pros and cons of an issue before coming down firmly for what he thought was right.

The Highlands and Islands Development Board asked Alastair to edit a book to mark the first twenty five years of its operations. When the book appeared in 1990 (*Highlands and Islands: a generation of progress*, Aberdeen University Press) Ken teased Alastair that the section on sport made no reference to game fishing and hunting, concentrating upon shinty, ski-ing, swimming and soccer. Alastair drew Ken's attention to a few lines in the late Professor George Houston's chapter on the land. "One enduring aspect of sport in the Highlands is the social division between the traditional pursuits of the very rich and the less costly recreations enjoyed by a much larger number of the less wealthy. In recent years Highland estates with access to salmon rivers, grouse moors and most of all stags, have doubled or even trebled their market value. The right to shoot one stag and acquire its antlers (but not its venison) can now cost the same as buying twenty blackface lambs. As the agricultural use of land brings in lower net returns, its sporting use has become much more profitable." Clearly Alastair valued the hills for walking not stalking, and doubted the real benefit to Highlanders which might be derived from hunting.

Quite recently Alastair had the responsibility of disposing of the effects of a very elderly aunt according to the wishes she and her late husband Archie Hyslop had expressed, or according to his own judgement if he had no such clear directions. Archie Hyslop was a very interesting character. Among other talents he had produced the lyrics for the songs which Harry Gordon, the music hall star, had built in to his comedy act. He had also been the moving spirit in the Aberdeen University Unionist Association as an undergraduate, when the association campaigned and won a rectorial election with Winston Churchill as a candidate. Churchill was probably the only rector who never delivered a rectorial address, and the reason for this is made clear in a bundle of papers which Alastair passed to me for the University. Amongst these papers was a telegram addressed to the president of the Aberdeen University Unionist Association, sent from Whitehall and dated 3.24pm, November 7, 1914. It reads: "I am deeply grateful to you for the honour you have conferred upon me and I shall endeavour to serve your interests to the best of my ability. The only thought in our minds in this present time must be the unflinching prosecution of the war by land and sea." In 1946, with two world wars behind him, Churchill received an honorary degree from the university. Later the university thanked Alastair for a very valuable addition to its archives.

As the reader will see, our associations with Alastair (and with Sheila) have been various and always rewarding. There are many more memories to relate but we have tried to illustrate their range and the light they shed upon the qualities of this remarkable man. On Ken's seventieth birthday Sheila and Alastair presented him with a magnificent four volume collection of Scottish poetry which has given much pleasure to us in the last six years. One couplet of Burns' provides a conspectus of how we view the amity and the affinity we have with the Hetheringtons:

How grand in age, how fair in youth,
Are holy 'Friendship, Love, and Truth'

Dad

Alastair's children

Lucy

Sunday morning. Sitting in front of a large industrial green pencil sharpener, turning the handle and watching in fascination through its glass window as curls of wood shavings appear inside. With pride I pull out another spike of sharp lead at the end of another muddy orange 2HB. In the course of the last week dad's blunted quite a few pencils – 2HBs and 2Bs as well – filling notebooks and no doubt making jottings in lots of margins. It is a special pleasure to sit on the floor of his attic study looking after the tools of the trade.

He, meanwhile, is on the 'phone. It's a reassuringly solid Sixties model with a rounded handset. He spends most of Sunday mornings talking into it and listening with a look of keen concentration. Often dad's end of the conversation is incomprehensible – a strange code to the small lieutenant on his floor. But that he's a general is clear to this admiring child. His tone is forceful and he talks in strategic terms. He loves to plot and to plan, to marshal his forces for a big campaign.

Maps are one of dad's great passions. The glass-cased cabinets in his desk are crammed full of Ordnance Surveys covering the whole of Britain. In front of him sit both the open *Times Atlas* and a *True to Life Globe*. As the conversation moves from country to country, from conflict to conflict, he charts its course with an accurate spin. Coups in Africa; dictatorships in South America; civil rights in the States; above all, the Bomb and the Cold War. And then out there beyond, lunar exploration and extra-terrestrial possibilities. The detail of what he says is lost on me but the excitement and energy are clear.

At some point, probably around noon, he'll break for a stride across Blackheath and Greenwich Park. Some of the family follow in tow. It's hard to keep up with dad and the emphasis is on exercise and invigoration rather than chat. Our destination is the statue of General Wolfe with its commanding view across London. It's not quite the Highland panorama he'd like but it's an imposing scene all the same. He stands and surveys the landscape stretched out before him, but it's to the horizon that his eye is most drawn.

On the way home we'll sometimes play games or run races. When he relaxes a little, dad likes to romp about – to give us piggy-backs or tickle us until we scream. He also loves to tell stories, true ones or ones that he makes up to entertain us. And he asks about our teachers and friends; he's interested in our aspirations on the toy front as well as in life.

Back home, the gong sounds and dad heads for the terrace outside the dining-room. As mum prepares the Sunday roast, dad performs his 30 "full knee-bends" to the booming sound of *The World This Weekend*.

Sundays with dad draw to a close over a large and sumptuous family lunch: meat and potatoes, stuffing and gravy before the office. Someone is usually naughty and has to be told off. There may be a row. But as the sense of well-being spreads from our mouths to our stomachs we're drawn together as a family. And dad, who loves puddings most of all, finishes his weekend at home with a look of extreme satisfaction relaxing his face and lighting up his eyes.

Tom

After breakfast one morning at Borwick Fold, dad got me to go with him to a quiet spot, armed with pens and artists' paper. We had guests staying at the Lakeland farmhouse where we took our holidays, and our day out was going to Ullswater for a picnic, where we would walk or take the boat from Glenridding to Howtown. My task was to help him plot the logistics, using the boat timetable and taking account of the walking abilities of those in the party. It was a typical idea – dad's enthusiasm for a project and his desire for me to have a go at working out a plan. The resulting day out was great as well!

During the Lakeland holidays in the Sixties and early Seventies, he was keen for us to join him on the mountains, but it was never forced. A wise tactic, leaving me in adult life with a great love of the hills and dales. These holidays – my main chance to see him as a child – were much more than mountains, though. He took up golf when I discovered the game with Scott, his brother, and we had many happy days on the courses at Windermere and Arran. As a child I knew he had an important job, but it was never made into a big deal. The Christmas cards from Harold and Ted went straight onto the mantelpiece without comment. I tried to persuade him which way to vote in the 1974 election without really noticing it was on the strength of his leading articles that I might have come to my conclusions.

With four Scottish grandparents I have always had a sense of Celtic blood in my veins. On a camping trip in the mid-Seventies, however, I appalled him by failing to recognise the Scottish flag flying over the National Trust visitor centre in Glencoe. I soon learned a little history. The night by the burn was typical – dad had no desire for fancy hotels when he knew the ideal camping site in the glen – but we ate well on good-quality steak cooked on the camp fire that night.

The independent spirit, passion, and determination have been picked up by my ten-year-old daughter, Natasha. She is insisting she and I should undertake a 350-mile day trip to Arran to climb Goatfell, and I am delighted to go along with this eccentric and exciting plan.

Mary

Pulling away from Stirling station in the train yesterday, it struck me that it was probably the first time in twenty-two years that I was leaving Scotland without dad being there to wave me off. Even in March, his expression rather blank but his eyes searching the train windows, he stood there with Sheila and waved as he had done so very many times before. Whether at a train station, airport or Brodick harbour, our goodbyes had so often been moments of emotion when his tenderness and sadness suddenly shone through and I felt the weight of feelings that had gone unexpressed. These glimpses on station platforms, the sudden ache of love and sense of loss, are ones I'm strangely glad of.

Even before he moved back to Scotland in 1976, we saw little of dad when we were growing up. During the week he was the mystery man who came in the middle of the night and had a thermos flask of cocoa awaiting him. He was the owner and organiser of the polished chest of drawers with its tub of Nivea and small compartment of change (occasionally pilfered), of the desk in his study with its pencils and sharpener, its paperweight and plastic calendar with an irresistible button to press which flipped the day and date on to the next. I loved to play with it but would then have to spend hours flipping through all the days and months until I got back to where I started.

Weekends and holidays meant walks and meals together, but we never quite had enough contact to bridge the gap completely. A father born on Hallowe'en was bound to have a certain mystique, however, and for many years I believed that this magical man who only darkened our door at midnight had special powers other fathers could barely dream of.

Ironically enough for an other-worldly wizard he appeared to be terrified of the Daleks in *Dr Who* and I took great delight in watching him hide behind the sofa when they trundled onto the screen. At that time he still called me "Little Mary". Once I had grown a bit more he would hedge his bets by addressing both of his daughters as "Lucy-Mary".

This haziness over what was close to home was characteristic of dad whose deep blue eyes so often seemed set on the horizon.

He could name all the peaks on the skyline as he gazed out from a mountaintop in Scotland or the Lakes, and his passion for them was infectious, but he didn't always discern when his enthusiasms weren't shared. Many's the person who has been swept along on his walks and hasn't liked to demur, only to hear themselves described as a keen climber whose defining characteristic is their fondness for the fells!

Memorable was the day when a large party including all of his children and grandchildren struggled up a hill behind dad finally to reach a picnic spot with a sufficiently impressive view. By now starving, we all eagerly unwrapped the dozens of sandwiches dad had been kind enough to prepare while we'd all loafed in bed that morning. "What's in them?", asked Tom.

"Stilton and marmalade," came the reply, just in the nick of time. Poor dad's chirpy enthusiasm turned to dismay as a collective cry of disgust went out and ten hungry faces turned to him in horror. It hadn't occurred to him that others might not appreciate what he deemed so delicious. Deeply puzzled that his family should be so perverse, he polished off as many as he could and then led the party down again with the copious leftovers in his knapsack.

Many memories of dad are tied to walks and food – not always combined although sharing Mars Bars is an enduring one. I can see him in his kitchen in Glasgow preparing steak and strawberries with swift efficiency; his fatherly concern if ever pudding was refused ("What? Are you ill?"); jumping onto the boat and crossing over to Arran for a Pelligrini's ice cream.

Later on I would have liked him to see in me the kind of bright-eyed, clean-living, accomplished daughter he wanted and deserved, but there was no disguising the low-achieving London adolescent I was. To some extent, however, he was protected by his innocence. On one of his visits to London my scarf slipped to reveal a purple bruise on my neck. I tried to cover it and reassure dad as fast as possible but he was anxious to examine the glaring lovebite and discover how his dear daughter had come by such an injury. Even Lucy and Alex's guffaws didn't alert him and for once I was grateful that my father, so in touch with world affairs, was rather endearingly out-of-touch with his teenage children.

Alex

Tramping two steps behind dad, picking our way across the marsh with boots that just leaked a little, in order to get to the place that was still quite a long way from the bottom of Sca Fell Pike. Wondering whether the bit where the hill disappeared into the cloud was near the top, or whether Helvellyn was so big that we would come out in the bright magical cloud land above. Wiping the sweat from my forehead and wishing that I'd drunk ten times more at that tiny stream well behind us now and wondering why grown-ups never got thirsty. There are countless memories of starting out on walks in fair weather and foul, in Scotland and England, on mountains that I knew the names of and on those that I could only marvel that anyone could pronounce.

Starting out was always the hard bit, the pain that came before the gain. If I was to attain the glory of the summit – whether it be in the distant hazy views of pikes and fells lit by the sun and swept by the breeze, or the fun of finding the next cairn high on a ridge but deep in the mist before the last cairn slipped out of sight – then I needed sustenance. The sustenance came from stories. I longed for them in the long silent trudge and one story was told over and over again to my wonder and awe, its increasing familiarity never decreasing my pleasure. Crossing the river to secure a bridgehead into Antwerp was better than any tale in any movie; not only daring but real, not only real but my dad! To be out ahead of the advancing allied armies, to disguise your tanks as the enemy's with camouflage, to face your cannon the wrong way firing at targets that were not really there, drive at top speed to kick up a dust storm and so straight past the German guards over a rickety bridge into the city. No wonder I wanted to hear it again and again. How much of what I remember was the history told and how much was my young imagination working as hard as the young legs going uphill I cannot tell, but of all the stories of childhood and of dad's army days that's the one I demanded most.

Years later I read a more detailed, though slightly less colourful account of the same event in dad's own words reproduced in Mark Arnold Forster's *The World at War*. Having stumbled across this by complete chance I was gripped to follow my private story again, alarmed at it being revealed to the whole world but filled with pride at each turning page. When I went next to Scotland I was full of my discovery: had dad heard of Mark Arnold Forster? Did he know that the story was in it? Yes, he had, indeed he knew him. Yes he knew the version of the story in the book and could show me others from his file of cuttings. I couldn't surprise him, but I could delight in the adventure once more.

Fifty years after its liberation he went with Sheila to Antwerp once more. The photos of a modern city he returned with could only dispel the images in my mind. However, the importance to him of the occasion and his pleasure at the reunion with Robert Vekemans, the man who led him to the bridge fifty years before, were in accord with my pleasure and my sense of the importance of his role in that piece of history.

Part II

By Alastair

Throughout his journalistic career, Alastair kept a meticulous record of his own work in a succession of cuttings books, the first of which, the Marcus Ward, made in Belfast, is described as "a ready reference receptacle for Scraps of Print, from our chief sources of knowledge – the Newspapers".

These cuttings, thousands in number and spanning forty years, start with a short article for the Glasgow *Evening Times* about his initial rejection for military service and end with pieces for his local paper, the *Arran Banner*, written in retirement at High Corrie.

The selection of material that follows falls into three categories. First, there is a thrilling narrative about his wartime exploits. Then I have chosen excerpts from the many leaders he wrote for the *Guardian*. One is published in full – his blistering attack on the British government for its misadventure in Suez. Others, though abbreviated for reasons of space, fairly represent his view of the post-war world. The book ends appropriately with articles by Alastair about his native Scotland.

K.R.

I: Alastair's war

To Field Marshal Montgomery and the Allied Commanders, almost three months after D-Day, the liberation of Antwerp was a matter of urgency. Supplies for the armies as they began the advance into Germany still had to be transported from the Normandy ports. The great docks at Antwerp would provide a fast supply route for desperately needed fuel, equipment and provisions. Their capture – in a usable condition – was vital.

In early September 1944 those docks were the immediate target of the 11th British Armoured Division, under the command of a brilliant young general, Philip Roberts. The Germans were waiting in strength, prepared and determined to defend the city and the docks with all their might: the battle for Antwerp was expected to be the most difficult and dangerous operation since the Normandy landings.

In the end it was not. That, above all, was thanks to the initiative and courage of a Belgian civil engineer, Robert Vekemans, who by his heroic action saved hundreds of British lives and permitted the taking of the docks both quickly and intact. He was later awarded the Military Cross by Montgomery – the only non-British person ever to receive the award.

Vekemans had served as a lieutenant in the Belgian Royal Engineers. In 1940, during the British Army's retreat from Flanders, he was taken prisoner and sent to Germany. Because of his professional qualifications, the Germans returned him to Belgium after four months, to repair war-damaged bridges. Since then he had been employed by the Belgian public works department. He was a member of the Resistance group "Secret Army" and active in the Action Information Service "Alex".

On the afternoon of September 3, having been illegally listening to the BBC in his flat in Antwerp, Vekemans correctly deduced that the British forces must be close to the Belgian border. (In fact the leading tanks and armoured cars had crossed near Tournai that afternoon.)

Vekemans went to have a meeting with the harbourmaster, whom he knew well. He learned that the Germans had called for pilots and crews for five block ships, which were to sail by the first tide next day, to be sunk across the harbour entrances in the River Scheldt. He told the harbourmaster that a delay of even one tide could be vital and suggested that it would be useful if the pilots failed to arrive in time. Fail they did. The block ships were never put into position.

At about 5pm Vekemans took a tram to the town of Boom, about fourteen miles south of Antwerp. He had correctly guessed that this would be the line taken by the British tanks, since a direct approach from the west would bring them to the wrong side of the River Scheldt, more than half a mile wide at Antwerp.

As he left the city he observed that German guns, barbed wire and minefields were in place on the defence belt to the south, but that the main road itself had not yet been mined. At Boom, where the road crosses the River Rupel (at this point about the width of the Thames at Westminster) there was a further defence belt. The great bridge across the river was defended by guns, wire, mines and booby traps. Two hundred yards further south, beside the canal, German infantry were dug in along the forward defence positions.

Vekemans took a look at the Germans on the main bridge and was warned off by a guard. He then walked about 400 yards up-river, to a much older bridge – the Van Escholdt bridge, built in 1852. This was wide enough for only one vehicle and in poor condition, though still in use. He found it less well guarded, though demolition charges were in place. He noted that the Bickford wick with the main spring cord leading to the charges ran along the upstream balustrade of the bridge.

Showing his official pass, Vekemans talked a soldier into allowing him to walk across the bridge and on to the village of Willebroek, about two miles to the south. Here he contacted a shipyard worker (a former corporal in his army unit) for more information, and then walked seven miles along the canal to his mother-in-law's house, where he spent the night listening to the BBC and gathering information about German movements in the area.

At dawn next day he cycled back down the canal, left his bicycle at the corporal's house, and went into a cafe. Its shutters were closed, but he persuaded the proprietor to open one up, so that he could watch the road from the south. He had chosen this spot after carefully calculating the field of view from the forward German positions. If his plan was to work, he would have to stop the leading tanks well before they came into view of the German positions south of Boom. He was very uncertain that he would be able to stop the tanks, however. He expected a long wait.

To his astonishment, only half an hour after he had settled down, Vekemans saw a column of British tanks coming up from the south. He went out and stood in the road with his arms raised – a lonely figure in a grey mackintosh. As he had feared, the first tank rumbled up with turret closed, refused to stop, by-passed him and moved on.

The second tank, however slowed down. Its commander stuck his head out and pointed back to the fourth tank in the group. This was the Squadron Leader's tank – that of Major John Dunlop of the Third Royal Tanks. It stopped. Dunlop, dark and bearded, gestured with his pistol that Vekemans should climb up and say what he had to say.

Vekemans was urgent and convincing, asking Dunlop to stop the advance of the leading tanks before the Germans could sight them, and explaining in English that if the column continued up the road they would come under heavy fire and the bridge would be blown. He put forward a plan of his own, suggesting that instead they should turn off by a side road to the smaller bridge. He believed that this bridge could be rushed, and he would guide them if they were willing.

Something about Vekemans's manner – his quiet determination, his detailed description of what lay ahead – convinced John Dunlop. The squadron turned off along the dusty little road. Vekemans was put in a scout car and led the way through the village of Willebroek, crossing the canal and leaving three tanks to guard the crossing. The other tanks turned north, along the canal bank. A few thousand yards short of the Van Escholdt Bridge they stopped behind a factory wall. There, at Vekemans's suggestion, the leading tanks turned their guns to face backwards and covered their British marking with camouflage nets.

After a final briefing by Vekemans, three tanks went ahead,

Lieutenant Gibson Stubbs in the lead. Robert Vekemans followed in a scout car, John Dunlop in his tank behind him. The tanks went flat out for the bridge, kicking up as much dust as possible.

The ruse worked. In the dust, noise and confusion, the Germans beside the bridge mistook them for their own tanks. The first British tank was across the bridge and beside the houses on the far side before a shot was fired.

Vekemans in the scout car wanted to stop in the middle of the bridge. Not surprisingly, the driver, conscious that the bridge might be blown up at any moment, did not, and tried to drive on. Vekemans seized him by the collar, shouting "Stop! I must cut the wire!" As the car came to a halt, Vekemans jumped out, carrying a knife. With machine-gun fire now coming at them from both sides of the bridge, Vekemans sliced through the wire in two places and ran back to where the demolition charges were, to make sure there was no other hand primer, found none, and rejoined the scout car.

As soon as they were across, the second and third tanks opened fire. Having gained the north shore, the tanks drove swiftly through the street and turned back onto the main bridge, taking the Germans completely by surprise. There was a sharp battle, but the bridge was captured with far fewer casualties than if the column had driven from the south straight into the trap that awaited them.

During the battle the bridge itself was damaged, and the remaining fourteen tanks, waiting on the southern shore, crossed the Rupel by the Van Escholdt bridge, while Royal Engineers set about repairing the main bridge.

I mention my own part in this affair only because it was rather surprising (to me). In retrospect there was perhaps an element of farce about part of it. But September 4, 1944, turned out to be an extraordinary day in my life. As an Intelligence Officer, I was with the tanks as they approached Boom. The advance through France had been so fast that maps of Antwerp had not caught up with us. About ten o'clock I was sent to Mechelen, ten miles away, now (it was thought) in the hands of the 23rd Hussars, to pick up what maps I could find. My driver and I shot off, drove through the narrow streets of the old town into the market square, and stopped at the entrance to the beautiful mediaeval Town House.

The great door was closed, but a horrified official stuck his head out and whispered hoarsely "What are you doing here! Look, look! The Germans are all here!" Yards away, across the square, lined up and ready to go into Antwerp, were German infantry, tanks and armoured cars. Fortunately the quick-thinking official opened up the door and let our car into the courtyard. I spent twenty minutes or so sorting out maps in an office upstairs. He put his head out, observed that the Germans were facing in the opposite direction, and opened the doors for us. We sped out of Mechelen faster than we had entered it, and returned to Boom.

About noon a force of tanks, infantry and engineers set off northwards, while others remained to clear the Germans from the canal and riverbanks. Robert Vekemans travelled with the commanding officer, Colonel Silvertop. About two miles along the road the column ran into fierce German defence. There was another sharp battle and some of our men were killed.

Here Vekemans performed his next great service. At one o'clock he and Colonel Silvertop had a short telephone conference with General Roberts. Vekemans suggested that as they came out to the outskirts of Antwerp those tanks heading for the docks should skirt the city centre, avoiding the area round the Central Park, where the Germans had concentrated troops in strong defensive positions, with bunker shelters. He offered to guide the tanks by back streets.

Colonel Silvertop meantime led a squadron into the city, where fierce fighting took place near the Central Park during the afternoon and evening. Six thousand astonished Germans were taken prisoner and (for want of anywhere else to put them) temporarily interned in the Zoo beside the railway station.

My route maps were not needed, though detailed maps of the docks would have been invaluable to Pip Roberts that night. Vekemans guided the advance, and by mid-afternoon British tanks were moving fast through the back streets of the city to the main lock gates and sluices. Once again the Germans were taken by surprise. Their commander later complained that he had not expected us for at least two more days – which, but for

Vekemans, would have been the case. There had been no time, therefore, for them to carry out the planned demolition of the docks.

Vekemans followed the leading tanks as they entered the docks, and I was able to follow a little further behind. At one point, perhaps unwisely, I drove alone beside the river to assess the situation, and came under close fire from Germans on the opposite bank as they began to realise what was happening. Tanks making for the wharves were attacked from kerbside pillboxes. During the night there was heavy fighting. By the next day 11th Armoured Division, greatly assisted by members of the Resistance, had carried out Montgomery's order to take Antwerp docks intact.

Much more was to come. It would take a further two months and the loss of many Allied lives to clear the estuary of the Scheldt and allow the port to be used. And Antwerp would be devastated by German rocket attacks and many thousands of its citizens killed.

But that afternoon I took Vekemans to meet General Roberts and we called at the headquarters of the Secret Army. Afterwards, Vekemans turned to me politely and said, "And now, let us go to my home. You will have a cup of tea and meet my wife". And we did.

Anyone visiting Boom and Willebroek today would find many changes. The Van Escholdt Bridge has gone, the lovely old main bridge has been replaced, and a road tunnel runs under the river. But on the Willebroek shore, at the place where the tanks began their crossing of the Van Escholdt Bridge, there sits a Sherman tank with an inscription recounting the heroism of Robert Vekemans.

[Sheila Hetherington adds the following footnote: In September 1994, Alastair and I were invited to Antwerp as guests of the burgermeester for the week-long celebrations marking the fiftieth anniversary of the city's liberation. Robert Vekemans was there (as was a very aged Pip Roberts). One afternoon, with Robert and his wife, we drove up to Willebroek for the small town's own celebrations. The entire community was congregated beside the tank, together with the town band; and we were late, as Robert had lost the way. I slipped to the back of the crowd, conscious that I had played no part in the liberation, so was far away from Alastair when I heard Robert end his speech by saying, unexpectedly, "And now, my friends, Major Hetherington will address you." Alastair was already unwell with the illness that now afflicts him so sadly, and I was stunned – but I need not have been anxious. Alastair rose to the occasion delightfully, paying a short tribute to Robert, to his own former comrades, and to all the citizens of Willebroek, who responded with enormous cheers, before the band left the scene.]

II: Alastair's *Guardian* leaders

Suez

The Anglo-French ultimatum to Egypt is an act of folly, without justification in any terms but brief expediency. It pours petrol on a growing fire. There is no knowing what kind of explosion will follow. There was, admittedly, about one chance in twenty that it might put out the fire. By sheer weight it might have extinguished the flames, temporarily at least. But it is far more likely to lead Britain into direct war with Egypt, and perhaps with the whole Arab world – as, on the latest reports, it seems to be doing. What is more, countless other nations will consider Britain and France to be in the wrong. As the two governments must have known, it was exceedingly improbable that Egypt would withdraw its forces to the west of the canal. Why should it, except possibly through fear of fighting Britain? Already it is engaged with the Israelis east of the canal and in the Sinai desert. If they are withdrawing from their grandiose raid – which for them would be the only sensible course, militarily and politically – the Egyptian command will want to pursue them and harass them as they go. For the Egyptian forces to retreat behind the canal, one hundred miles inside their frontier, would be an admission of defeat. In the present mood of Egypt – of the government, army, and people – it was most unlikely to happen. In the event, Egypt has rejected the ultimatum. It declines to retreat. So it appears probable that at dawn this morning, or soon afterwards, the British assault force will land in Egypt.

The Prime Minister sought to justify the ultimatum by saying that we must protect our shipping, our citizens, and "vital international rights". But what possible right have we to attack another country? The British and French military action threatened in the ultimatum, if carried out, will be flagrant aggression. Protection of shipping – or for that matter of rights of transit through the Suez Canal – is no cause for making war, unless it is done with the authority of the United Nations. Nor can an assault on another country be warranted on the ground that we wish to safeguard the lives of British and French citizens. (In fact our action is likely to place them in greater jeopardy.) Nothing in the charter, or in acknowledged international law, permits armed intervention in such a cause. As for the "vital international rights" of which Sir Anthony [Eden] speaks, what are they? The first right which we ought to be protecting, and the first duty which we ought to respect, is the rule of law. Instead Britain and France are taking the law into their own hands. Again, admittedly, there is a slender chance that by today's dawn the Security Council will have authorised intervention. But, in face of a probable Soviet veto and of the known views of other countries, the chance is so slender that the British and French Governments could not remotely count on it. They have acted in a rash and precipitate fashion. To much of the world they will appear to have seized upon the shallowest excuse to reoccupy the canal zone, as they wanted to do weeks ago. The Prime Minister says that no other course is open to us. He is gravely mistaken. The proper course would have been to call on Israel, through the Security Council, to withdraw its forces immediately to its own territory. At the same time both Egypt and Israel should have been reminded of the tripartite declaration (which Sir Anthony, in his first statement to the House, seems to have overlooked). This would have been the way to promote peace. Instead the Government has taken us well on the way to a bigger war.

The Anglo-French action is the more shocking when it is realised that the Israeli action appeared near its end. The raid had not turned into a full-scale campaign, nor did it look like doing so. The evidence, of course, is uncertain. The Foreign Secretary has spoken of increasing air action yesterday afternoon and of the danger that fighting would soon take place on the canal. But there are strong indications that the Israeli operation was conceived as a raid, very heavy and spectacular, but with limited objectives. (Even if it had been something greater, Britain could not invoke the Anglo-Egyptian treaty of 1954 to reoccupy its Suez bases, since an attack by Israel on Egypt is specifically excluded from being a reason for British reoccupation.) The Israeli foreign ministry now says that the purpose of the raid was only to wipe out the large fedayeen (or commando) units in the Sinai desert. The explanation is fairly plausible. After an interval during the Suez crisis, the fedayeen had begun to maraud again across the Israeli border in a most brutal way. Even among those who condemn Israel for its excessive reprisals there is recognition that Israel's patience has been put to a terrible test. But the raid towards Suez has been a most dangerous move – and it seems likely to bring Israel into still greater difficulties. At present the best thing the Israel Government can do is to get its troops back within their borders. The sooner it does so the better. The longer the present Israeli operation continues the more danger there will be of other Arab States joining in. The Israel Government ought by now to grasp the point that if it holds on in Egyptian territory it will be buying successes today at the expense of ruin tomorrow. But, as must be bitterly acknowledged, the British and French Governments are following a similar path. Yesterday's events – and today's – are all too likely to have a tragic ending for the West.

October 31, 1956

Macmillan

From the immediate point of view of the Conservative Party, Mr Macmillan is the best possible choice for Prime Minister. It is less certain, however, that he is the best choice either for the party's long-term prospects or for the country's well-being. That he will be a competent Prime Minister no one need doubt. He has done well as a departmental Minister successively in Housing, Defence, the Foreign Office and the Treasury. That is a wide range to have covered in five years – too wide, perhaps, for the benefit of individual departments, but valuable in a man now called to the highest office – and in each appointment he has left behind him a good reputation and a record of achievement. He has, in addition, a flair and on occasions a fire which can stir people to a belief in his leadership. These are strong assets. But he comes in with one grave disadvantage. It is that he represents the Right, the backward-looking element in the Conservative Party. That is, of course, precisely why he is the best immediate choice for the party. He can hold the party together – an acrobatic feat in which others might have crashed.

January 11, 1957

Television

The BBC at least is following the advice given by the chairman of the Independent Television Authority. In its autumn programmes for television, it is not letting itself drift with the popular tide. It has announced a brave experiment in putting more solid content into its programmes. This, in effect, is what Sir Kenneth Clark proposed to the independent companies in his speech a week ago. He rightly said that the audience research figures could be dangerous weapons if used solely with an eye to quick returns. As he put it:

> The companies, it seems to me, have the responsibility of choosing programmes which nourish life rather than those which allow us to drift away from it into a kind of melodious coma or a world of reassuring unreality.

This surely is what the BBC intends to do by dropping the more fatuous of "quiz" programmes and panel games. It is keeping on those with an element of mental agility and a turn of wit, such as *Animal, Vegetable and Mineral*. It is both bidding for popularity through a steady diet of light entertainment and plays – what it calls "a star light entertainment show" will be on the air every night – and at the same time it is providing a bigger diet of news, serious features, and discussion. No doubt some of its items will be as mawkish as anything on anyone's network, but the hard reality will be there too (even if it is Wilfred Pickles brilliantly telling a story by J. B. Priestley). So far the audience figures have been against the BBC. Its programmes do not appear at all in the latest "top ten" ratings. But, with courage, its spokesman says that the BBC does not believe it will necessarily lose the mass audience by putting on more adult programmes.

September 7, 1957

The bomb

The French have decided to join the nuclear club. They have started to make their own bombs. They are likely to test one within the next eighteen months. They can, of course, put forward exactly the same arguments as the British, for they, too, want to influence Washington and to insure themselves. There is a measure of justification in this, just as there is for Britain; although certainly for the French, and probably for the British, the prestige and power are sought for their own sake. After France, who will come next? It may be Sweden or Israel or Japan. And with each new entrant to the nuclear field the risk that these weapons may be used increases...This is the competition which ought to be stopped now. Britain, by volunteering to renounce her separate possession of nuclear weapons in return for an agreement that nobody else will start making them, could lead the way. Russia and the United States can stay outside such an agreement at present; plainly the process of negotiating nuclear disarmament for them will be long. But can the Government not seek a rapid treaty with all other nations?

February 14, 1958

General Election, 1959

Under Mr Gaitskell, the ghosts of austerity have been exorcised; it is no longer a sin for a Socialist to want a car and a holiday abroad. To its credit, however, Labour has not slackened its social conscience. It wants to use prosperity to help the needy and to extend social services. The promise of higher pensions, better hospitals, and more new schools is not the "bribery" that it has been called: it is less selfish than the kind of appeal underlying "Life's better with the Conservatives". We should not vote simply for our own stomachs, but for a fair distribution of extra wealth...Our view, then, is that in a straight fight Labour is to be preferred to the Conservatives. But in three-cornered contests, the Liberals deserve support except when their chances are negligible and Labour's are good.

October 7, 1959

[The Conservatives won]

Labour splits

Although he [Aneurin Bevan] talked of a united party, it did not seem one after his speech. The party is not certain to go onwards now to the modernisation of policy for which Mr Gaitskell asked. It may do so: we hope that it will. But the prospect is not plain. What Mr Gaitskell sought must appear, to outsiders, to be elementary – that the party constitution should be brought up to date. Its only specific statement of essentials, he said, concerns "the common ownership of the means of production, distribution, and exchange". It makes no reference at all to colonial freedom, race relations, disarmament, full employment, or planning. Therefore he wants it rewritten. To most people this may be simple common sense; but to some at the conference it was accursed.

November 30, 1959

The Queen's children

The Queen's explanation [in her Christmas broadcast] of why she did not want her children to appear with her on television was gently worded; but it may be recalled that, earlier this year, her press secretary had to tell the Press Council that "the private lives of the Royal Family were being increasingly disrupted by certain sections of the press". That arose particularly from the persistence of a few newspapers in trying to obtain titbits from Cheam School about the Prince of Wales. There has been some improvement; but for that, the hope of giving the Prince a normal education would have diminished. The aim of letting him have a normal life is a good one, and it should not be disrupted for the sake of providing back-page gossip.

December 27, 1959

Lady Chatterley

It remains a matter of astonishment that the prosecution was ever brought. Many books of a more doubtful character are on open sale – books devoted to promiscuity, prostitution, sadism, incest, and sex with violence. Many of these are written in a brutally cold-blooded way, without either the tenderness of *Lady Chatterley's Lover* or its literary merit. They degrade sex where Lawrence elevates it. Yet their publishers go unprosecuted. Perhaps they do no great harm; that is a matter of opinion. But if anyone was to be prosecuted, why pick on Penguin Books and *Lady Chatterley's Lover*? Someone seems to have blundered in the office of the Director of Public Prosecutions or of the Attorney-General. The jury, however, have shown more sense.

November 3, 1960

Conscription

National Service has claimed its last men. After those who entered the forces on Thursday, no more are to be called. Thus, when Thursday's intake emerges in 1962, an unloved institution will end. National Service was necessary, but the gross misuse of conscripts by the Army was not. Many millions of man-hours have been wasted through the complacency and incompetence of the War Office and of lower commands. The Navy and the RAF have not been above reproach in their use of men, but they have never been so irresponsible as parts of the Army. The training of recruits has been symptomatic of the ills common in the Army's approach. Even when rearmament was most urgent, in the days of the Korean war and of the Rhine Army's expansion under Eisenhower, tank crews were spending seven or eight times as long on drill parades as on the essentials of tank driving or tank gunnery. They were being shipped overseas – and perhaps still are – with boots which shone superbly and with belts blancoed to perfection, but with only a scanty knowledge of the skills that mean life or death in action.

November 19, 1960

Europe

The vision which inspired Britain's approach to Europe was of prosperity and peace – prosperity through access to the large market, and peace through leadership of a new Great Power. We must not lose sight of that vision; nor should we be so blinded by it that we fail to look at whether it can be accomplished. As yet the economic reckoning cannot be completed. Politically the prospect of leadership exists; but only if Britain is ready for a close political union in Europe. On this Mr Macmillan was not completely candid on Saturday. He said that "there is no question of our being asked or expected to accept any system of a federal character". If he had added the words "at this stage" he would have been near the truth; but before long we shall almost certainly be asked to accept something like a federal system. If we want to share in the leadership of Europe, we must be ready for this.

October 15, 1962

Cuba

Wisely, President Kennedy has accepted the Russian retreat with quiet words. Jubilation could have wrecked what little chance there is of turning the crisis to constructive use. No doubt plenty of Americans will cry "chicken" after Mr Khruschev. But in the White House it seems to be understood that an appalling catastrophe has just been escaped. That is as well – both because the crisis may turn out to have done some injury to America's own reputation for peaceful conduct, and because vital negotiations lie ahead. One consequence of the past week's alarm could be to give fresh energy to the disarmament negotiations. It would be logical if both sides were to take warning from their recent nearness to nuclear war, and were to work seriously again for a general disarmament agreement. The withdrawal of overseas military bases, by stages, has its place in this; so do nuclear free zones. To expect quick progress after the long deadlock on disarmament would be foolish, but both sides, having been at the brink of annihilation, may have come back with clearer minds.

October 29, 1962

The death of Gaitskell

He would have been a better Prime Minister than Leader of the Opposition, because his talents were creative. Already, as

Minister of Fuel and briefly as Chancellor of the Exchequer, he had shown his ability for organisation and administration. As Leader of the Opposition, he was more concerned with seeking constructive policies – looking towards the day when Labour would again be in office – than with negatively damning the Government. He was too fair-minded not to see the truth of a situation and he knew that the freedom of any Government is circumscribed by events, by its allies, and by its physical resources. He rarely, if ever, took unfair advantage of the licence that an Opposition can exploit. Personally, too, it could be said of him that in opposition he was too kind to some of his critics within the party. He never waged the kind of personal warfare that some of his closest colleagues waged against him.

January 19, 1963

The Profumo scandal

Mr Macmillan and his Government may be about to go. If so, those who for years have been critical of him will not be sorry. But at least some of us will be sorry if he is forced out for the wrong reasons. The charge of "moral corruption" against Mr Macmillan and his Cabinet is unproved. One Minister lied, lived immorally, and perhaps took risks with security. It does not follow either that Mr Macmillan knew of this or that his colleagues condoned Mr Profumo's behaviour. Much can be said against Mr Macmillan's handling of the affair, especially because of his failure so far to let anyone outside the Government examine the security aspects and the possible involvement of other Ministers. If he does not remedy that failure on Monday, he will deserve the strongest censure. But, if he is forced out because of unproved moral charges, his successor, whether Conservative or Labour, will build on sand. A new Conservative Government would still be under suspicion. A new Labour Government would have got in without clear public support for its policies.

June 14, 1963

Sir Alec

His background is not one of his assets. To hold an ancient earldom, to have been brought up in ancestral privilege, and to have been the proprietor of great estates is no longer a commendation...Already Lord Home is suspect among internationally minded voters because of his ambiguous attitude to the United Nations. Among those who also look for an urgent advance in rehousing, urban renewal, and the replanning of our densely packed industrial communities, he must be equally suspect until he has proved himself. As a true Tory he is acceptable to the Cavendishes; but it is as a progressive Conservative that he has to make himself acceptable to Parliament and the public.

October 19, 1963

Britain

Perth, too, has its slums. Within half a mile of the market where the Prime Minister first stated his Government's priorities – economic expansion, a modern Britain, the spreading of prosperity – there are crowded tenements with four dwellings sharing a single lavatory. These are conditions which no one now ought to tolerate. In a prosperous county town such as Perth they are exceptional, and only a few people have to endure them. In many of Britain's industrial areas they are not so exceptional. Nearly a third of Manchester's citizens – a quarter of a million people – today are living in condemned dwellings. In Liverpool, Leeds, Glasgow and other cities the record is not much better. In smaller boroughs it is sometimes worse. Large tracts of Northern England, Central Scotland and South Wales are squalid and, in a strict sense, uncivilised. Mile follows mile of dingy streets, dirty factories, and filthy air – with only an occasional tree, park, or open prospect. To say that the North of England contains some of the finest scenery in the world is only a slight recompense. People have to live their daily lives in the towns and cities.

Improvement is taking place, but not quickly enough. To

bring home what urban life too often means, in human terms, the *Guardian* six weeks ago began its articles on "A New Britain" with a report on a family in Drum Street, Openshaw. The Bennetts have lived in Openshaw all their lives. They are not discontented and they do not grumble. They are better off than they were ten years ago, and they can afford summer holidays in Cornwall. They now have hot running water in the house, though no bathroom and only an outside lavatory. Their son goes to a well built modern school, though one where classes are large and teachers tend not to stay. They long, nevertheless, to live in a place which is cleaner, where the shops are not strung out along a main trunk road, where you do not see a factory wall the moment you get out of bed, and where the social divisions are less marked. There are millions of others in Britain like the Bennetts.

November 4, 1963

The death of Kennedy

He will be remembered, as much as anything, for his youth and friendliness. "The torch has been passed to a new generation of Americans," he said in his inaugural address. To people in many other countries it was gladdening to see leading the greatest of Western nations a young man, though one matured by war and by years of public service. He and Mrs Kennedy made the White House what it had hardly ever been before – a place where artists and thinkers of all nations and creeds were welcomed. He was a true liberal, a thinker no less than a man of action, and a courageous leader.

November 23, 1963

General Election, 1964

Labour has been elected because it has a creative programme. It has offered a fresh approach to economic growth, efficiency and prosperity. It has offered social justice as the basis of an incomes policy, which in turn is a means towards restraining inflation. It has offered to set vigorously about the task of rebuilding our cities and improving our physical surroundings. It has offered to try to make Britain's voice better heard at the centre of the Atlantic alliance – and in the United Nations and in international diplomacy. The latest trade figures, the changes in Moscow, and the Chinese bomb all emphasise the urgency of the tasks. Most of what it wants to do can be done without exposing itself to prolonged Parliamentary battles. Mr Wilson wants to get on with the job. It is waiting for him – and more than half the nation wants him to get on with it.

October 17, 1964

Rhodesia

Is reconciliation with the Smith regime acceptable? If the illegal declaration of independence were the only count against Mr Smith's Government, reconciliation would be possible. We must look, however, at the kind of society that the Rhodesian Front was creating long before UDI. It not only denied Africans political advancement; it denied them social and economic advancement. They could not own land or farm in many of the richest parts of the country. They could not live with their families near the centres of cities unless they were domestic servants. Their movement was subject to restrictions, and outside the tribal areas their life was closely watched by the police. Their children's prospects of more than a simple form of primary education were slight, although in other African countries secondary education is expanding fast. Every form of political activity, of public meeting, or of journalism was controlled. All this happened before UDI; all this would be perpetuated under any Rhodesian Front Government. Is this the kind of society that Mr Heath [Leader of the Opposition] is ready to tolerate?...It is unwise of Mr Wilson, however strong the pressure in Parliament, to rule out any thought of British military action. By March or April, he may be faced with a situation in which if Britain does not invade Rhodesia others will do it for her – and with bloodier consequences.

December 22, 1965

The Wilson Government

What is wrong with the Labour Party – with the Government and its backbenchers? Not just a bit of backbiting from the Prime Minister, nor a row over defence. Not just the stress of uncertainty over the Common Market, nor disagreement about decimal currency. Something more fundamental has gone wrong – and has been missed in the acres of weekend commentary. It is the eclipse of Labour's idealism.

March 6, 1967

Vietnam

The revulsion against the war is not only because of bombing in the North. It is as much because of the death, destruction, and apparent failure in the South. Many Americans are asking, as well they may, about the morality of their country's conduct. Among young people, already the most disaffected, opposition continues to spread. For President Johnson, the problem is both moral and practical. It is how to explain America's conduct in terms that will go some way towards satisfying moral scruples in one group of objectors and yet convince the others that there remains a prospect of success in South Vietnam...But President Johnson dithers, fumbles, and changes his mind, giving the generals at times a freedom that his Defence Secretary would not allow them. Also, the Texas politician in the President seems barely capable of discerning a moral issue when one faces him.

August 30, 1967

Paris 1968

Yes, it could happen here. Not for the same reasons as in France, nor as quickly. Perhaps not with the same degree of violence (though, thanks to great self-discipline among students and workers, the casualties in France have so far been astonishingly small). But something similar could happen here. The ingredients exist. Both the established political parties are distrusted because of failure while in office. The reputation of Parliament itself has suffered because it spends so much time on party back-biting and because it seems unable to influence events. And in politics there is a trend towards polarisation – with the Conservatives under pressure to move to the Right, while the effective leadership on the Left has shifted to student radicals and others outside Parliament. Another acute economic crisis could strain our system severely.

Fortunately there are moderating factors here. Selfish though most of us are, a greater sense of community exists in Britain than is common in large countries. It is no accident that the Welfare State was evolved in Britain and has become an accepted part of British life. The tradition of political toleration and free speech also goes deep (though how deep has not really been tested for more than twenty years). In Britain people have been able to express their resentments publicly, even though they have not been able to get the action they want from successive Governments. And the racial problem, although potentially explosive, is not numerically as serious as in the United States.

May 27, 1968

Europe, again

The Prime Minister is still trying to lead Britain haltingly into Europe. But what sort of Europe? Not the dynamic democracy towards which many of us have long wanted to look, but a Europe that is little more than the Brussels-managed bureaucracy of today. If the European concept is worth pursuing – and it is – then it must be as a living political union. It must also be as a political union in which democratic control of the common institutions is clearly established. On this, what has the Prime Minister to say? Having built up hope by talking of his "aspirations" for a "greater and more effective political union", he let them down again in his Guildhall speech last night by saying that no supra-national federal or political arrangements could become a reality within ten or twenty years.

Such, once again, is the tame and shuffling approach of British Governments to Europe.

July 30, 1969

Ireland

Internment without trial is hateful, repressive, and undemocratic. In the existing Irish situation, most regrettably, it is also inevitable. Shooting, bombing, and burning now occur every day. The men responsible generally disappear, unidentified. Through fear or through misplaced loyalty, others will not say what they have seen. Northern Ireland's economic life, already tottering, is being brought further towards bankruptcy. Tension between the Protestant and Catholic communities is being fanned into bitter hatred. The army, trying to keep the peace, is placed under intolerable strain. To remove the ringleaders, in the hope that the atmosphere may calm down, is a step to which there is no obvious alternative. It will not work quickly, and it may not work at all. To succeed it will have to be backed by other political and economic measures. But it represents the only immediate hope of preventing a total catastrophe in Ireland.

August 10, 1971

Bloody Sunday

This tragedy again throws into relief the apparently endless Irish problem. Is Ulster to be seen only as a land of bigoted Protestants facing rebellious Catholics? Or as a land of beleaguered Protestants who will not be coerced into joining the South facing alienated Catholics who have never accepted the North? How far is its poverty responsible for the depth of its divisions and misery?

Events like yesterday's must delay and make immensely more difficult the approach to a peaceful settlement. Yet a settlement must be approached. The majority of Catholics and Protestants would probably by far prefer to live at peace and on tolerant terms with their neighbours. For the British, too, a peaceful solution would be a vast relief....

In the end, the last word will lie with Irishmen. They deserve a future that breaks away from the hatreds and miseries of the past. This is surely what most want, in spite of their Orange and Green feuds. If Irishmen on either side choose to follow diehard leaders, they will take an inexorable path to a more terrible future. If the IRA are allowed to lead the Catholics, the fighting will grow more intense. If uncompromising Unionists are allowed to lead the Protestants, then they may find that they are left by the British to fend for themselves. Either of these extremes will take Ireland into civil war. In that event, internment will begin to look like a polite Sunday school picnic. So will yesterday's disaster in Londonderry. It will be a tragedy worse than any that Ireland has seen yet. The British responsibility is to try to prevent it, which means that we, too, have to keep cool heads.

January 31, 1972

Mrs Thatcher

Apart from not mandatorily ending "eleven plus" segregation, Mrs Thatcher [Education Secretary] is more than half way towards a respectably Socialist education policy. Whatever Mr Short or his successor may say, yesterday's White Paper is sensibly progressive.

December 7, 1972

Vietnam, again

The strategy now adopted by President Nixon in Vietnam is horrifying. Heavy bombing has been resumed against targets throughout North Vietnam...It is the action of a man blinded by fury or incapable of seeing the consequences of what he is doing. Does Mr Nixon want to go down in history as one of the most murderous and bloodthirsty of American Presidents? Has he any concept of how he will end the war? For end it he must.

To unleash the bombing again with full ferocity is a grave error even from his own viewpoint. Far from strengthening the American bargaining position, it will convince many people inside and outside the United States that unconditional withdrawal is now the only course. The President must be left in no doubt that his action is abhorrent.

December 20, 1972

The death of LBJ

Having worked as a youth administrator in Roosevelt's New Deal, he knew the suffering of poor families and the unemployed. He was closer to the harshness of life than John Kennedy, a rich New Englander, could ever be. He used all his gifts in mobilising public opinion, cajoling Congress, and picking men to help him get the poverty programme going – and it brought new jobs, housing, medical care, and social security payments for the poor. In civil rights he took over Kennedy's measures, pressed them, and refused concessions to the "white backlash" in the South. Although a Southerner himself, he was determined that blacks should be equal citizens. Perhaps nearly all white Americans were too slow to accept reform, but Johnson was less slow than most.

January 24, 1973

The miners' strike

The NUM may no longer care that it is seen as a bully. Last time it struck, the miners benefited from much public sympathy. This time the ban on overtime has brought little. This is not through lack of understanding that working underground is dangerous and disagreeable, but because the NUM is proving exceptionally greedy.

November 26, 1973

General Election, February 1974

Logically, the situation points to a Grand Coalition of all three parties, possibly with Mr Thorpe at its head. Although it is unlikely to come about, it would represent the nearest approach to what the public appears to want.

March 4, 1974

The closed shop

The Secretary for Employment [Michael Foot] is sowing the seeds of conflict. When he was in Fleet Street thirty years ago, the NUJ was largely a professional association. Even in 1971, the date to which Mr Foot wants to turn the calendar back, the NUJ would not have contemplated "blacking" the work of non-union writers or restricting them to a narrow ration of one contribution every six months. If that kind of action becomes common, it will destroy one of the public purposes for which newspapers exist. It will stop everyone from MPs to ornithologists from writing except infrequently. That is where Mr Foot is leading us.

January 22, 1975

Mrs Thatcher, again

For Mr Wilson the choice of Mrs Thatcher as his opponent cannot be comforting. She will savage when it suits her, and she will not be easily put down. But can she achieve the status of a potential Prime Minister?...She is no Golda Meir or Indira Gandhi – not yet, at least. It will need all her shrewdness and common sense to keep the Conservatives on the Disraelian course that she says she admires.

February 12, 1975

Europe, finally

The result [of the Referendum] is unambiguous. Britain wants to remain in the Common Market. It is a tonic for Britain and a tonic for Europe...The whole United Kingdom has two or three extremely tough years ahead. It will not regret yesterday's decision. In Europe, Britain's future is likely to prove both more prosperous and more secure. We shall have to work hard to improve our own prospects. But the referendum result is a watershed successfully crossed.

June 7, 1975

III: Alastair on Scotland

Jean's hut

One morning last week a strange sight was to be seen on the Cairngorm path. A man was making his way up the mountain with a step-ladder strapped to his back. He was not, like the Alpine pioneers, going to scale cliffs with it, nor was he, like the Victorian inhabitants of Braemar, intent on making Ben Macdhui the highest mountain in Britain. The purpose of the ladder was evident by the evening. High on the slopes of Cairngorm itself a hut had appeared. From the foot of the mountain its silvery roof was just evident to the eye, and with a telescope its sturdy green walls were also visible. Next day the man with the ladder was down the mountain again, his job done.

Of course, the building of the hut was shared among many people, and its sudden erection in a single day was the result of long preparation. But why build on the mountain at all? Briefly, to provide shelter at an approach to our most massive group of high hills. Four of the Cairngorm summits rise above four thousand feet, and many square miles of their plateau stand near that height. It is an area of sub-Arctic conditions and extreme remoteness. That is its attraction and its danger.

On Wednesday the men working at the hut could sit shirtless in the warm sun. The mountains had an Arcadian calm. On Thursday the Arctic blast had come. The gale drove before it black squalls, each bringing a shattering volley of rain. The hut shook and the weather streamed from its rhones. But already, on the first day of the hut's life, it was a refuge to which climbers struggling on the plateau could think of turning. If the storm became impossible or night caught them on the top, the hut was there to help them. And at least one party that day was glad to know that it was there.

Soon the first snow of winter will fall. The last drifts from last winter still linger, grey and dirty, in the corrie above the hut. By November the skiers will be back in the Cairngorms, threading their way up the ridges, working across the plateau, and racing down the corries. It is to them that the hut will be of the greatest value. Coire Cas, in which it stands, has become a favourite skiing ground since the war. In spring it frequently gives a downhill run of more than two miles straight. As late as June this year – an exceptional year – a continuous ribbon of snow still stretched a mile from the plateau at 3,900 feet to the site of the hut at about 2,500 feet.

The hut is a memorial to a skier. The plaque for its door reads:

> In memory of Jean McIntyre Smith,
> who trod this way joyfully –
> Cha till i tuilidh.

The Gaelic words mean "She will not return". Jean Smith was killed in Coire Cas in the spring of 1948, and the hut is a gift from her father, a Hebridean doctor.

Many people have helped to build Jean's hut. Permission came from the Forestry Commission and Inverness County Council. The work was organised by Glenmore Lodge, the Scottish Centre of Outdoor Training. The building was prefabricated in sections by a firm in Glasgow. It was taken by lorry to the end of the road beyond Loch Morlich. From there the sections had to be hauled on sledges through a forest, over a steep glacial moraine, and up the mountainside.

Most of the hauling was done by school-children from Glasgow and Lanarkshire attending special courses at Glenmore Lodge. It was part of their training in outdoor life and in meeting the challenge of the hills. And a fierce challenge it must have been in the early spring. Parties of boys and girls aged fifteen and sixteen camped out for a week at a time to help in moving the sections. With snow and wind it was hard camping, so hard that one night the tents were blown down in a gale. But they seem to have enjoyed it – certainly it was a change from city schools. "Gie me Argyle Street" was one girl's comment, but hers was not the common view.

Men and women from Glenmore Lodge prepared the site in July and August, levelling the ground and concreting the foundations. Then last week the hut was erected. For this, two professional carpenters came from Glasgow to direct the amateurs. They thought the climbers quite mad to want to live in such a place, though they themselves slept one night on the mountain and sang as loud as any round the fire. When they saw the weather on Thursday morning they shook their heads to all offers of a climb and took the first train back to the city.

The interior has still to be fitted out, as has the porch. The porch is important because it will house the mountain rescue kit and stretcher. Its doors will always be unlocked, and in emergencies four or five people could sleep on its floor.

Jean's hut is an outpost on the north side of the Cairngorms. To the south lies Corrour bothy, rebuilt last year also by voluntary effort. These are the only buildings in twenty miles of magnificent mountains. There is a third recognised refuge – the shelter stone at the head of Loch Avon, a gloomy cavern in a grim setting. Three shelters in such an area are not many. Nor can they become the gin palaces which some people have feared (though a little rum would never go amiss on a night at any of them). They are spartan places, fitting their setting.

Each has its own character. Corrour bothy is said to take its matronly primness from the wise old hinds who graze in the corries above it – or, perhaps, from the granite-like Aberdonians who rebuilt it. The shelter stone is bleak and cheerless, surrounded by the stoniest slabs and crags in the Cairngorms – a contrast with the rich Alpine grasslands on the plateau above. It has a sense of lurking disquiet, a legacy of the murderers who once hid there. What will be the character of Jean's hut? From Jean surely something will come, so that others also may tread joyfully through Coire Cas. And perhaps also something from Clach Bharraig, the great boulder which stands some way below it. To geologists Clach Bharraig is a perched block; to Gaels it is the fairy stone. May the fairies of Glenmore Forest give Jean's hut good luck.

Glasgow Herald, September 19, 1951

The Question of Scotland

Scottish issues, as such, are unimportant. "Dead as a dodo" was one Conservative comment in Lanarkshire, and a Labour speaker in Dunbartonshire said: "Scottish questions? We don't get any." They are, nevertheless, being raised at some meetings to the obvious boredom of audiences.

Reporting the 1951 General Election campaign for the Glasgow Herald, October 22, 1951

Exile

By the waters of Babylon they sat down and wept, when they remembered Zion. By the Mersey, Aire, and Trent we don't exactly weep. We just grind our teeth a little at the thought of having left Scotland. The authors of Psalm 137, after all, were taken in captivity. We went of our own free will – and, thank goodness, we can escape to the clear Scottish air two or three times a year when we wish. Dr Johnson had it all wrong. The finest sight a Scotsman ever saw was the night sleeper northwards. You get into it in the gloom of a Manchester or Wigan evening and wake up early next morning with the sun raising the curlew above Beattock or behind Gleneagles. Or, as I have done more often lately, you can leave by road in the small hours, cross Shap with the dawn, breakfast at Dumfries or Crawford, and be in Glasgow or Edinburgh in time to meet friends over morning coffee.

Yet how many of us expatriates would go back to work in Scotland? It is hard to tell. It depends so much on the kind of work one wants to do and on the chance circumstance of opportunities. The great draw of England, as of farther lands, is that it is bigger, pays better, and offers greater scope. My own concern is with newspapers. Scotland has good newspapers, but England has better. The average standard in Scotland is higher than in England, but the peak in the south is loftier than in the north. Words written in Fleet Street or Cross Street are more likely to have an influence towards the peace and prosperity of our times (even if only a small one) than words written off Buchanan Street or behind Waverley. So it must be with some other professions. In reverse of the psalmist's words, it may be easier to sing the Lord's song in a strange land.

Still, in exile one appreciates more than ever the great advantages of Scotland. Sometimes one wonders, perhaps with a touch of envy, whether the Scots at home see the assets of their country as clearly as do those who have gone away. A spell of living under the grey shadow of the Pennines, where even the grass and rock twenty miles outside the city are black with grime, sharpens one's taste for the dignity of Glasgow and splendour of Edinburgh. (Yes, dignity: for even the tenements have a massiveness, the shipyards a towering strength, and the whole city a way of opening in sudden vistas such as the industrial middle of England does not know.) Then, too, a spell of working among people whose farthest horizon is bounded by Blackpool and Llandudno makes one wish for the encounters – so likely in any office or workshop in central Scotland – with men whose cousins are in Canada and parents in Argyll or Inverness. The Lancastrians are good, sturdy, reliable people; perhaps in some ways more direct and exact on the job than anyone touched with the Celtic twilight. Yet one misses the occasional softness of speech, the chance reference to some remote place, and the latent understanding that all men do not live as we do. In a Scottish group, even if most may have been born and bred in Lanarkshire or Midlothian, they know well that there are other worlds and other ways of life.

Scotland is at once compact and spacious. Compact in that its population is concentrated in the narrow central belt; spacious in having the great uplands beyond. Compactness means that people are interested in their country as a whole. Talk to a man in Motherwell about the new oil refineries at Grangemouth, and he will listen; he can visualise the place, even if he has been no nearer than on the train to Easter Road, and he has some concern for its relation to himself. Talk to a man from Huddersfield about the new refineries at Stanlow, on the Mersey, and you might as well speak of the moon. He is familiar with what lies immediately around him, and, as Frank Singleton has said in another context, he will either love it or hate it but not be neutral; industrial England, however, is too vast and too diffuse for him to appraise it with the same concern. So, again, there is a breadth of outlook and range of vision in Scotland which the southrons often lack. Is this not partly because a Scotsman may physically see his country from side to side – from the Firth of Clyde to the Firth of Forth, as you can on a clear day from Ben Lomond or the Campsies or (almost, but not quite) from Arthur's Seat? Denis Brogan once noted that Glasgow was the only city in Britain where, for some weeks, the leading newspaper was likely to carry a correspondence on whether the Paps of Jura were visible from the city. (To prevent a revival of that controversy, could I say that Jura is not to be seen but the hills of Arran easily are?)

Another Scottish asset, not always recognised so clearly at home as abroad, is the possession of a national church. The Church of Scotland is that much more than the Church of England. Not only in numbers, proportionate to the whole people, but also through the democracy of its government. These words appear in Assembly week, when men and women from all the presbyteries in Scotland are gathered in Edinburgh to discuss their church and nation. They sit with clergy and laity together, not separate. They can discuss freely whatever subjects they wish. They are bound by no outside power – for not even the Queen's representative, the Lord High Commissioner, can take his place until the Assembly has constituted itself and elected its moderator. No Act of Parliament lays down a liturgy or prohibits freedom of worship. The Scottish Book of Common Order begins by saying that it is for the guidance of ministers but should not be taken as restricting their freedom in the conduct of services; the English Prayer Book begins with the Act of Uniformity. There is a shrewd democracy, too, in the presbyterian doctrine of the priesthood of all believers. It identifies the church most fully with its people, and the people with the church.

An allied asset is Scottish education. It was a surprise to school teachers in England, during the recent debate on salaries, to find that their Scottish colleagues were better paid. But the Scots for long have given special attention to their schools and universities. Scotland had four universities when England had only two, and a limited post-war experience of Gilmorehill suggested to me that, as an all round *universitas*, it was more educative than English redbrick. If burning midnight electricity is any indication – either of social stimulation or of academic intentness – Glasgow wins easily over Manchester. It is a blaze of light on a winter evening when much of Manchester's premises are dark.

A breadth of outlook, a democratic church, and a sturdy background of educated minds – can these Scottish assets be turned more strongly to the British benefit? Brains are always said to have been a major Scottish export. Why not courage and morality as well? This, as has been said, is Assembly week. For the Assembly, of course, it is difficult to judge how far to go into secular fields. It does not want to overstep the bounds of its Christian duty. Yet one remembers its declaration last year against an unlimited continuation of hydrogen bomb experiments, because of the hazard to unborn generations – a declaration which no broadly based and responsible body in England had found itself able to make before that time. Perhaps this year on Cyprus we may hope for a similar clarity of leadership. It is an issue which threatens the good name of Britain throughout the world and confuses our friends abroad about Britain's true purpose. The Archbishop of Canterbury has spoken with a lonely voice on the side of conciliation and a Christian approach. The Assembly can give him powerful support. It is a body which can debate these issues freely, without partisan feeling, and with moral principle foremost in its mind. So, too, with other perplexities. The urge to get rich quick – by football pools, or premium bonds, or industrial feather-bedding – is coming to dominate the British outlook. In the shoddy surroundings which so many of our urban dwellers must endure, that is not too surprising. But we must find our way back to a healthier attitude. Scotland contains all the elements of the problem and the means to its solution. It could show the way forward to the rest of Britain. Is it doing so?

The Spectator, May 25, 1956

An old song

On March 19, 1707, the Scottish Estates in Edinburgh received an "exemplification" under the Great Seal of England of the Act of Union, lately passed at Westminster. They themselves had passed their Act at the beginning of the year, in spite of anti-Union riots in Glasgow and Edinburgh and a ceremonial burning of the Articles of Union in Dumfries. Now they were meeting almost for the last time. The Scottish Parliament finally dispersed a week later, on March 25, and has never since then assembled.

What force or guile could not subdue
Thro' many warlike ages
Is wrought now by a coward few
For hireling traitors wages

So Burns wrote, looking back from near the end of the century. The slander was not truly justified, but it has stuck. The choice for Scottish statesmen was between continuing poverty and the hope of prosperity, through free trade with the expanding English colonies. But the occasion, on March 19, was not without emotion. George Lockhart of Carnwath, the Member for Midlothian, recorded that Lord Seafield handed the exemplification to the Lord Clerk Register with a "despising and contemptuous remark" – "Now there's ane end of ane auld sang." But, as others have said, he may well have covered in a brusquely Scottish way his underlying sentiments. The song, however, was ended; and if it was not "Farewell to a' our Scottish fame", as Burns alleged, it was nevertheless the passing of an age which Edinburgh has ever since regretted. The Act came into force on May 1, and in October the first Union parliament met at Westminster. For long afterwards, of course, the Union was blamed for all Scotland's ills. Bailie Nicol Jarvie, we are told, even had to upbraid Andrew Fairservice when he "chose to impute the accident of one of the horses casting his shoe to the deteriorating influence of the Union". But, as the bailie said then and as might sometimes be recalled today, "Whisht, sir! Whisht! It's ill-scraped tongues like yours that make mischief between neighbourhoods and nations."

The Guardian, March 19, 1957

Closures on the Clyde

This is not a question of some small lame duck. It affects the future life and prosperity of one of Britain's greatest industrial areas. Unless the rescue [of Upper Clyde Shipbuilders] is thorough and effective, Clydeside is about to be turned into the blackest spot in a country with too many deprived districts. It will be worse off than the worst of Northern Ireland. The Government rightly wishes to make British industry more efficient and more competitive. But when that policy is carried ruthlessly to the point of destroying the basis of a whole productive community – one which has contributed a great deal to Britain in the past – then it becomes self-defeating. Mr Heath's Government ought to be planting new life and new prosperity in the heart of West Central Scotland, not a destructive cancer.

The Guardian, August 3, 1971

North Sea oil

For a fee of £6,250 the Occidental oil group two years ago obtained a licence to explore one area south-east of Orkney, now known to be among the richest undersea oilfields yet discovered. For further payments totalling £62,250 it can exploit that oilfield at a profit running into hundreds of millions of pounds. Tax on the profits will now have to be paid. Royalties at twelve and a half per cent of production values will also have to be paid. That will still leave Occidental – like other oil companies – with a gigantic profit. The extent to which the British Government has given away oil rights dirt cheap is shown by Occidental's Piper field. Although the Government could have been the piper itself, it did not call the tune.

The Guardian, March 12, 1973

Devolution

Mr Jo Grimond suggested some time ago that the first stage of devolution should be a ten-year experiment with a Scottish Parliament. This would control Scottish domestic affairs and some aspects of trade and industry, while the UK Parliament maintained its management of defence, foreign affairs, and the major aspects of economic policy. A constructive experiment on these lines seems called for. Goodwill, not conflict, should guide it. Bannockburn is rightly engraved in Scottish memory, but it is barely relevant in an age of high technology.

The Guardian, June 1, 1974

Muckle Flugga to Barra Head

In all the jubilation over the [European] referendum result, some thought should be given to why Shetland and the Western Isles voted "no". It was not some quixotic Norse response. It should be seen instead as a distress signal to Brussels, to London, and even to Edinburgh. These are the remotest constituencies anyway – far from the Scottish mainland and further still from the great centres of administration. They feel remote and separate. In addition, the decline in fishing, knitting and weaving so far has been less than offset by the coming of oil. The fishing fleets were and still are the biggest employers in both areas, but fewer boats are at sea and catches have shrunk. So have markets, for there is no longer a regular direct shipment of frozen fish from Lerwick to the United States. The fishermen and the boatbuilders are angry because the UK authorities have neither protected them from foreign competition nor negotiated an extension of fishing limits. In their eyes, part of the blame falls on the EEC, though non-EEC competitors are as great a threat.

Oil, of course, is bringing new prosperity – more so in Shetland than, as yet, in the Outer Hebrides. But oil also brings an alien way of life. After years of feeling left behind by twentieth century culture, the islands are having it suddenly thrust upon them, and many of their people do not like it. Though nobody objects to being better off, crofters and fishermen can resent the materialism of the new developments. And, particularly in Lewis and Harris, Presbyterians can resent the lack of respect for the sabbath. Mainlanders may be amazed that such attitudes survive. For the remoter islands, however, catching up with contemporary life is not all painless pleasure.

The Norse element comes in, too, for Shetland has a close affinity with Norway (which voted "no"). Also, Thursday's weather was evidently vile in the far north, which partly accounts for the poor turnout. Then there is the complex though probably irrelevant argument on whether Shetland should have "Faroese" status. That was a hare started by Scottish nationalists and pursued by a few Shetlanders, who stood on its head the slogan about "Scotland's oil". If it was "Shetland's oil", why were the Scots trying to take it away? The local evidence, however, suggests that this was never a serious issue. The decline of fishing, knitting and Harris Tweed is serious. It was once written that the Outer Hebrides "are the oldest-known splinter of Europe, their rock being almost wholly of Archaean gneiss". Politically, however, probably neither they nor the Shetlands want to remain splinters.

The Guardian, June 9, 1975

Lewis

Lewis is the northernmost of the Outer Hebrides and the most sternly Calvinistic. It is a place which, during the past 50 years, has changed probably less than anywhere in Britain. It is a place of paradox: of intense religion and intense alcoholism; of strict conformity on Sundays but of cheerful ceilidhs (with emotional singing and impromptu story-telling) on weekdays. It is a place where nearly all men are their own masters, each family living on its own croft, or smallholding, and free to decide its own daily routine; yet a place where social ostracism may come if you don't keep in line with accepted custom.

Sunday is rigorously observed. Walk through the streets of Stornoway at nine or ten on a Sunday morning, and they are empty, still and silent. Nobody is moving. It is as if all the people, incredibly, had been hidden away. Towards eleven they are out, in family groups, pacing their way or driving to church – most of all to the Free Church, where a congregation of 2,000 is not uncommon. Two-fifths, that is, of the town's entire population all worshipping together. You'll find nothing like that on the Scottish mainland, still less in England.

The island has antiquity, too, though not much evidence survives. At Callanish on the west coast, with a sea loch on three sides, stand some sixty tall stones laid out as a gigantic cross (although they are pre-Christian). Four thousand years ago, men put them there; men who must have had to struggle with wind and sea and poor soil as their descendants do today, on the Lewis crofts.

Over on the east coast of Lewis, for the past eighteen months, there has been a different kind of monolith: the high steel structure of a Drillmaster oilrig, undergoing conversion near Stornoway for BP, and due to move out to the Buchan field in May. A physical symbol of the twentieth century, work on the Drillmaster has brought to Lewis money such as has never been seen before.

That money has brought change – though less change than might have been expected, for the tough Calvinism of Lewis resists like rock. But, along with other influences, such as television and radio, and the return of men and women who have worked on the mainland, the new prosperity is having its effect.

You will encounter two fairly distinct views. Among elders and ministers of the churches, particularly the Free Church, you may find concern and anxiety lest the Lewis way of life and its dominant morality are undermined by wealth and by incoming workers. Among younger people and some shopkeepers, and even some teachers, you will find thankfulness that jobs and money are less scarce than they were, and that, for example, today's ceilidhs are enlivened by two or three successful local pop groups.

A middle view comes from Sandy Matheson, former provost of Stornoway, an elder of the Church of Scotland (here a minority beside the Free Church), proprietor of a pharmacy and bookshop and, as Labour candidate at the last general election, runner-up to the sitting MP, Donald Stewart. Sandy Matheson without hesitation welcomes the prosperity that work on the Drillmaster has brought, and he gives credit to the company, Lewis Offshore, for having played fair, by drawing half its employees from the island. As a magistrate, he says that there have been few signs of social friction, in spite of the influx of 600 or 700 mainland steelworkers and electricians. But he insists that the community's conventions, such as Sunday observance, must be respected.

A rather different view of the weekend can be found among the mainland men – many of them former shipyard workers from Clydeside and Tyneside. They earn on average £160 to £170 a week, for a sixty-hour, six-day week, but when they are not allowed to work, on Sundays, time hangs heavily. A few have fishing tackle and can escape to a discreet distance from habitation. The majority stay all day on their dormitory ship, reading or playing table tennis, and drinking nothing stronger than cider. (The local authority will not allow a licence on the ship.) Others stay quietly at lodgings in the town.

I was startled to hear from a group of workers on the Najla (the dormitory ship) that one Sunday about a year ago they had been stopped from playing football – not by the management or anyone else out at Arnish Point, but by the *police*, who explained that they had received a complaint and, as a matter of goodwill, were asking the footballers to desist on a Sunday. Which they did.

From the town of Stornoway it is a good mile and a half across the bay to Arnish Point, and about six miles by road. So someone with binoculars must have been watching from the town that Sunday to see the off-duty workers playing football beside the yard. One of the good elders or brethern of one of the churches must have been keeping watch, or an official of the Lord's Day Observance Society. "It's not the twentieth century up here," one of the Clydeside men remarked.

That apart, relations between incomers and inhabitants seem to have been good. Talking to some of the young Lewisian apprentices at Arnish Point, I found them appreciative of the coaching they had received from mainlanders; and they know that until now the only way to get the kind of training available at Arnish would have been to go to Glasgow. In the town, too, a couple of publicans confirmed that most of the drinking is three or four social pints even on a Saturday night. The problems with too many drams are mostly with the Lewismen, not with incomers.

One can understand, nevertheless, some of the anxiety over the presence of 600 or 700 outsiders – all of one sex – in a town of only just over 5,000 people. Even the big flow of money through the shops and through the households providing lodgings is seen as having disturbing effects. One elder remarked on a deterioration of manners in the shops of Stornoway, and of more bad language in the streets, though neither was immediately apparent to me.

Murdo Macritchie is the principal Free Church minister in Stornoway – and this year's Free Church Moderator for the whole of Scotland – and he says that the money is having both good and bad effects. When asked about behaviour in his own congregation, he replies that there has been no change. It is as good as it ever was, and the Sabbath is properly observed.

Is the Free Church not too strict? Must young people incur the censure of the elders if, having been to the long morning service, they go walking in the country on a Sunday afternoon? Why not encourage them to enjoy the beauties of nature, with which Lewis is so richly endowed? Mr Macritchie replies that the Sabbath is for the worship of God, for evangelism and the teaching of others, and for promoting the cause of Christ. One ought to refrain from recreations that are lawful on other days. And (with a mild chuckle) he said that I would not be asking about what is permissible on Sundays if I knew my Catechism.

Maybe not, but I still think that modest enjoyment of the countryside on a Sunday afternoon does nobody any harm. It is at least as spiritual as doing what I know some Lewisians do, which is to go to bed or doze in an armchair until it is time for the evening service. Of course, one of the elders may come to call on you on a Sunday afternoon; they are diligent in their supervision.

One danger in the severity of Free Church discipline is that, sooner or later, young people "blast out". That phrase I take from Francis Thompson, author and teacher and a thoroughly loyal Lewis man, though less orthodox than some. As much as anyone, he wants to preserve the Lewis way of life, and he is ardent in the cause of Gaelic culture. But he recognises the strains imposed by strict conformity, and he would welcome a more tolerant attitude.

Francis Thompson speaks also of the danger inherent in the kind of double standard that led to closure of Stornoway's only cinema (indeed, the only cinema in the Outer Hebrides) when it was about to show *Jesus Christ Superstar* when, not long before, it had shown both *Emmanuelle* and *Clockwork Orange*. Miraculously, when the showing of *Jesus Christ Superstar* was imminent, the cinema's fire precautions were found to be defective and so the showing never took place. As Francis

Thompson says, alcoholism among young people is rightly condemned by the Free Church and by others, but it might be less prevalent if going to the pub was not usually the only recreation available.

He, too, has an ambivalent view about the prosperity brought by oil-related work in the past two or three years. Yes, it contributes towards better health, better housing, and better nutrition; but it has weakened the coherence of mutual help among neighbours in the Hebrides. And, yes, by letting young people earn good wages early in life it has freed them from over-dependence on their parents; but it has also broken family bonds that would have been better kept intact.

Lewis remains probably the most law-abiding and stable community in the British Isles. Apart from offences brought about by alcohol, the crime rate is almost non-existent. Standards of education are high, and most Lewis people who have gone to earn their living on the mainland would dearly like to return to the island if the number of jobs available and prosperity grow. While personally I might find the requirements of conformity a little oppressive, given a touch of liberalism that society could be one of the most attractive in which to live.

Some time ago I asked a Lewisman now working in Glasgow what he missed most: "Walking *past* the Free Church on a Sunday morning," he replied, "and hearing the singing from inside." I hope he'll go back to live there before too long and not feel guilty if he goes for a walk along the superb coast on a Sunday afternoon.

The Listener, March 20, 1980

Sunset over Sutherland

The *Northern Times*, of Golspie, Sutherland, has lately converted to new printing technology with none of the troubles that have plagued its better-known counterpart in London. It could well claim to be a Fleet Street paper, for the river Fleet in Sutherland is far grander than that London sewer and reputedly has 2,000 salmon a day going upriver in season. The editor of the *Northern Times*, an old friend, lives in a house that has the most beautiful outlook of any editor's that I know. It faces south at the narrows where Loch Fleet runs into the sea – the site of the old ferry, until Telford designed a new crossing three miles upstream. From the porch of his house we watched the sun go down over the nearest Sutherland hills, disturbed only by a screaming low-level flight of US F-111s on their way to the Tain bombing range. Mercifully they soon passed, leaving the oyster-catchers and the tide as the only sounds while night fell.

The Listener, August 26, 1982

Arran summer

The deer are feeling the heat, like the humans. Most summers they come down round our Arran cottage in the evenings and the grass outside the garden fence is cropped low. This year, it is about six inches high, and not a hind or stag has been seen at low level for a month. High in the corries they can be watched in peace, looking well fed and taking their ease on grassy patches. But we miss their evening visits, destructive though they sometimes are.

An unusual visitor blocked our neighbour's water supply – an eel. The filtering rose in the burn is old, and the eel must have found a way through it. It probably came from a bigger burn about 300 yards away, for knowledgeable people say that in hot weather eels can travel some distance across dry land in search of better streams. Adders we have quite often encountered while cutting peat on the moor, but this is the first eel. Fortunately, the water-supply, being fed by mountain springs, is still flowing well.

We are not cutting peat this year, though, because the moor is being fenced and forested. A helicopter has been over this week spraying it with "glyphosate" – or at least that's what the warning notice calls it. That will kill the bracken, which must be a good thing, but presumably it will also kill the heather, the rhododendrons, the thyme and the bog myrtle. A pity, for it was a pleasing moor.

The Listener, August 4, 1983

Hill-walking

Conventional wisdom says that the Pirnmill Hills, on the west of Arran, are just big round boring lumps. Quite wrong: for although they are part of a granite dome they have pleasing ridges and they include the island's finest high-level lochan. Red deer, red-throated divers, and a golden eagle (if you are lucky) are all to be seen. Above the coastal crofts, these hills have stood unchanged for thousands of years – and you won't meet many people on them.

Whether they qualify as a wilderness is arguable. With a westerly gale blowing off the Atlantic or when the cloud is down and careful compass work is required on the ridges, they are not easy. Eastwards there are neither tracks nor habitation for many miles. Only in a small sector to the south-west has man intruded, with forestry plantations. Even the sheep are few once you are above 1,000ft.

For years an uncle of mine had a cottage at Pirnmill, and it was the base for many expeditions. In high summer he thought nothing of going up Beinn Bharrain ("Varren") or Beinn Bhreac ("Vrack") before breakfast – three hours or so up and down. But to cover the whole stretch, south to north or north to south, is an all-day task. In winter the tops can be snow-covered for weeks on end, crisp or icy underfoot. In bad weather a crossing west-east to Catacol Glen or Glen Easan Biorach provided – and still provides – a rewarding day. And, of course, if you want a really long walk you can start from Lochranza and tackle Beinn Bhiorach and Beinn Tarsuinn (the lesser of two Arran hills with that name) before crossing over to the Pirnmill group – a round trip of over twenty miles.

The best way, in my view, is to leave Pirnmill by the path on the north side of the Gobhlach ("Go-lach") burn. Note the birch and hazel coppices as you go – good cover for birds – and the surviving beech hedges probably planted about 1850 on the orders of the eleventh Duke of Hamilton, one of Arran's few creative landlords. Higher up the Gobhlach burn you will see a sequence of fine little waterfalls as you climb to the open moorland.

There, cross the burn and head south-south-east, not for the prominent westerly ridge of Beinn Bharrain (though it will give you a good walk another day, leading to the rocky Casteal na h'Iolaire) but to the shorter and steeper middle ridge, leading almost directly to Bharrain's main peak. It provides some good, airy rock scrambling. It is steep at first, with easy slabs, but becomes narrower and more broken later. It is a miniature A'Chir, requiring care in places. If you wish, however, all the awkward places can be bypassed on the west side.

At the main top, only 2,368ft/721m above the sea but likely to feel higher, look west to the Atlantic. This is the greatest panorama of the day. On the Antrim coast of Ireland you can pick out Fair Head, and further to the west the mouth of Loch Foyle. Then to your west the islands of Islay and Jura, and to the north-west the summit of Ben More, Mull. In the foreground are Kintyre and the Kilbrannan Sound, with the Carradale fishing fleet at work and possibly a submarine or two in training.

Having viewed and rested, keep north-east and then north along the broad ridge to the second summit, Beinn Bhreac, 2,333ft/711m. It is here, or just beyond, that you stand the best chance of seeing a golden eagle, for they are thought to like the far side of Catacol Glen. Keep on northwards to a lesser hump with a prominent cairn, and from just beyond it you can look down past granite cliffs to Coire Fhionn Lochan, or colloquially Corrie Lochan to most Arran people, with a sandy beach and a dramatic setting which make it a popular walk from the clachan of Thundergay. The red-throated diver nests beside the loch; and in spring-time groups of geologists can also be seen on its shore (some of both sexes even swimming in the icy water).

If by now you have had enough, the descent by the lochan and the path to Thundergay is always pleasing. The ardent, however, will keep going northwards – past Meall Bhig to the day's final top, Meall nan Damh, which is no more than 1,870ft/570m but has an unbroken view northwards up Loch Fyne and to the Southern Highlands. Its north-eastern shoulder is adorned by another small stretch of silver water, Lochan a' Mhill, which you will almost certainly have to yourselves. Not sandy, but good for swimming on a hot day. You are, however, getting down into the territory of the midge, so in July and August prepare to be bitten.

Beware, finally, of the descent to Catacol village through the bracken. The birch woods are lovely and the bracken vile. Find a sheep track and follow it, for in summer the bracken can be as much as five feet high and exceedingly tiresome. The beach at Catacol is stony, so not good for swimming, but about one-and-a-half miles down the road back to Pirnmill there is a little sandy stretch just south of Rubha Airigh Bheirg. For campers there is good grass here, but no amenities.

A historic footnote: though the country inland is wild and empty, the thin strip of crofting land along the coast has long antecedents. From Beinn Bharrain and Beinn Bhreac you can see the Irish coast, not so very far away, and it was from Dalriada in the north of Ireland that the first "Scots" came to colonise south-west Scotland. Feargus, one of three brothers, became the ruler of Kintyre, Arran, Bute and other islands in the Clyde, while one of his brothers ruled Islay and Jura and another held Lorne and Mull. All that was in the sixth century, and all three owed loyalty to the Irish Dalriada. The main settlements were round Blackwaterfoot, Lochranza, Brodick and Lamlash.

In the seventh century a grandson of Feargus, Aiden MacGabhran, united the Scottish Dalriada into one kingdom, secured its separation from Ireland, and extended it as far as Stirling and Perth on the mainland. He is a lineal ancestor of the present royal family, and he was the first British monarch to be consecrated at his crowning (by Columba, in Iona). Think of him as you walk these hills. It is highly probable that he walked them too. Suidhe Fhearghas ("the seat of Feargus") above Glen Sannox takes its name from his grandfather.

From Wild Walks (Diadem Books, 1988)

Index